Encounters
With a
Supernatural
GOD

Angelic Visitations in the Night

Jim and Michal Ann Goll

Destiny Image® Publishers, Inc.
P.O. Box 310
Shippensburg, PA 17257-0310

"Tapping the Power of the Age to Come"

ISBN 1-56043-199-7

For Worldwide Distribution
Printed in the U.S.A.

This book and all other Destiny Image, Revival Press,
and Treasure House books are available
at Christian bookstores and distributors worldwide.

For a U.S. bookstore nearest you, call **1-800-722-6774**.
For more information on foreign distributors, call **717-532-3040**.
Visit the author's website at **http://www.reapernet.com/mttn**

Acknowledgments

Much gratitude goes to those who have tutored us over the years. The Lord has been so faithful to bring different mentors, tutors, peers, and friends into our lives just when we needed them. We bless the Lord for the teachers who grounded us; the pastors who cared for us; the evangelists who inspired us; the prophets who anointed us; the apostles who oversaw us; and the intercessors who have covered us. We dare not mention names—the list would be exhaustive! You know who you are. Bless you, and thank you.

We also wish to acknowledge and thank the Lord for the staff of Destiny Image. They are a rare breed of servant-leaders whose passion is to see that the message the Lord has given to others be broadcast far and wide. Thanks for adopting us into your family.

But we wish to dedicate this book, *Encounters With a Supernatural God*, to the next generation of emerging prophetic leaders in the Body of Christ. This book is written for you. May you be inspired from the recording of these visitations and the lessons enclosed and learn. May you, as young eagles of the Lord, grow strong in character and gifting and rise up and fulfill your destiny. May a generation of prophetic people called the Church come forth and give to the Lord the glory that is due His name. It is to you, young eagles, that we dedicate this book.

Endorsements

What they so movingly share in this book is transforming because they themselves have been transformed. They make us hungry, not so much to hear as they have heard or to see as they have seen, but to join them in becoming like the One they have beheld.

—**Stephen Mansfield, Senior Pastor**
Belmont Church, Nashville, Tennessee
Author of *Never Give In*

An engaging, dramatic, biblical, faith-building message of two people's encounters with God, His angels, and the Holy Spirit.

—**Mark Virkler, Ph.D., President**
Christian Leadership University, Buffalo, New York
Author of *Communion With God*

Jim and Michal Ann Goll have arrived at the wonderful balance of being both very biblically minded and highly prophetic. This book will be of immense encouragement and great help to those who what to live biblical, supernatural lifestyles in seeking and serving the Good Shepherd: Jesus of Nazareth!

—**Marc A. Dupont, Founder of Mantle of Praise Ministries**
Associate Pastor at Toronto Airport Christian Fellowship
Author of *The Church of the 3rd Millennium*

The authentic, faith-building encouragement contained in this book will change your expectation for the presence of God. The raw power that has carried Jim and Michal Ann Goll's ministry to over 30 nations will not let you put this book down.

—**Mickey Robinson, Founder of Seagate Ministries**
Director of Prophetic Christian Ministries, Jackson, Mississippi

Contents

Foreword

I have known Jim Goll for about a decade. Jim and Michal Ann have been a part of our last four prophetic conferences in St. Louis. They have been very helpful in equipping the hundreds who have attended in understanding the realm of the prophetic and the supernatural dimensions of Christianity. We have been blessed by their team teaching at the conferences, and now the general public can gain knowledge from their team writing on a much-needed subject. Our God is a supernatural God, and He and His angelic host are involved in supernatural actitivity on behalf of the Christian Church.

While ministering in Birmingham, England, I had opportunity to meet Omar Cabrerra. We met for several hours. It was so eye-opening to learn from him about the important role that angelic beings have had in his ministry. I remember he told me that we in North America understand the role of the Holy Spirit, but we haven't yet understood the role of angels in our battle against the enemy. Later, while in Argentina, I spent more time with Omar Cabrerra, and also with Carlos Anacondia. It would be true to say that some of the leaders in Latin America who have been used powerfully in revival have a much more supernatural worldview than those of us in North America. I believe that many of us in North America need to experience the reality of seeing our resources in the heavenlies, which includes the ministry of angels.

I personally read this book with great interest for God spoke to me this past year that I had accepted only part of the prophetic word that came to me the night before I went to Toronto Airport Christian Fellowship to preach (an event that changed my life). I believe that as I move into the part of the prophecy that I haven't yet experienced, my life will once again be greatly changed and my faith again increased. The prophecy I received on January 19, 1994, from a businessman in Texas (who had spoken into my life for the preceeding ten years with great accuracy) was as follows: "Test Me now, test Me now, test Me now. Do not be afraid; I will back you up. I want your eyes to be opened to see My resources for you in the heavenlies, just as Elisha prayed that Gehazi's eyes would be opened. Do not become anxious; when you become anxious, you can't hear Me." I believe that the ministry of angels is a significant part of the above prophecy. Jim and Michal Ann's book has encouraged me to continue desiring to experience the reality of this dimension.

Since I entered the biblical worldview and gave up my liberal, non-supernatural, closed worldview, I have repeatedly met people who had the ability to see into the dimension where angels and demons are visible. I myself have only once seen into that realm. However, Jim and Michal Ann are the only individuals I personally know who have been visited repeatedly by angels over a period of many days. I have met pastors in Russia who were visited during times of persecution. I have had a noted Southern Baptist professor who at the time was teaching at the Southern Baptist Theological Seminary, tell me of angels appearing in China and on one occasion protected the Christians from attack by communists. The Communist army was moving through the street toward the church when they suddenly turned and ran. Later it was discovered that many saw angels on the roof of the church, which so frightened the soldiers that they turned and ran.

It is with confidence and trust in the character of Jim and Michal Ann Goll that I recommend, as a great read, *Encounters With a Supernatural God: Angelic Visitations in the Night.*

Randy Clark
Senior Pastor, St. Louis Vineyard Christian Fellowship
Founder, Global Awakening

Introduction

This book, *Encounters With a Supernatural God*, is about the modern-day operation of signs, wonders, angelic visitations, visions, and dreams. This is not merely some science fiction glimpse into what things might look like and be like some day. It is not just a biblical exposé. Nor is it just a storybook of awesome, incredible experiences. This inspirational manual on Holy Spirit phenomena is taken straight from the lives of me and my wife, is biblically grounded, and is balanced by years of experience. In fact, this book is written primarily from my wife's perspective!

Let me personalize this. In the spring of 1991, a seasoned prophetic man named Bob Jones told me, "*Your wife is going to be one of the first 200 women who will be released into the prophetic.*" I filed that statement away, not knowing what to make of it. I had been moving in the revelatory gifts for several years at that point, but I had not seen my wife, Michal Ann, particularly moving in that direction. She had other giftings, of course. But it didn't seem like the prophetic arena was her territory. Then things changed in a major way—and our lives changed too!

God, in the form of a Holy Intruder, invaded our lives. It was October 6, 1992, the Day of Atonement. We were at home asleep. Suddenly, a lightning bolt struck in our backyard at 11:59 p.m. When I opened my eyes, a man was standing in our room. He looked at me and I looked at him for one minute, and then I heard, "*Watch your wife. I am about to speak to her.*" Sure enough, that night started a nine-week period of visitations that did not center around me, but around my dear wife, Michal Ann Goll. Life has never been the same—nor would I want it to be.

Earlier that same year, I was given a dream in which I was instructed to study the ministry and function of angels. I gave myself to that task and read every book I could find, read the 300-plus Scriptures in the Bible that reference angels, and dialogued with others who knew these realms. With fresh envisioning from the Scriptures now under our belt, we little expected what was next. But then it happened! Our house became a habitation of the angelic and supernatural expressions of the Holy Spirit. Michal Ann and I are convinced that those experiences were not just for us. These encounters were for you, the Body of Christ, to learn from, be inspired from, and glean lessons from. I am totally convinced that, as the period of time the Bible calls the "last days" proceeds, there will be an increase of encounters with a supernatural God.

The prophet Joel foretold of such days when the Holy Spirit would be poured out upon all flesh.

And it will come about after this that I will pour out My Spirit on all mankind; and your sons and daughters will prophesy, your old men will dream dreams, your young men will see visions. And even on your male and female servants I will pour out My Spirit in those days. And I will display wonders in the sky and on the earth, blood, fire, and columns of smoke (Joel 2:28-30).

Years later, Peter the apostle took his stand with the other 11 disciples of Jesus on the historic celebration of the Jewish Feast of Pentecost and claimed that those days were the beginning of the fulfillment of Joel's prophecy. But notice what he said would happen in that period of time called the "last days": God "will grant wonders in the sky above, and signs on the earth beneath" (Acts 2:19). Wow! What descriptive terms those are that portray the unfolding of history's changing, end-time events.

God is drawing near to His people in these days. Perhaps the old adage fits, "Ready or not, here I come!" Get ready, guys! The Holy Spirit is breaking out of our man-made religious boxes and is showing up in diverse, awe-inspiring ways.

Have you been crying out for greater intimacy with Christ? Have you been asking for His presence to draw near? Do you desire to see His raw power displayed? Do you want to see Jesus receive the rewards for His suffering? Then watch out! You are a prime target for an invasion. If these questions echo the sounds of your heart, then I have news for you: This book has been written just for you.

Jim W. Goll

Chapter 1

Visitations in the Night

Michal Ann Goll

And Moses said, I will now turn aside, and see this great sight... (Exodus 3:3 KJV).

I'll never forget the night in November of 1992 when my husband, Jim, looked at me from the other side of our kitchen and said, *"I don't know who you are, and I don't know who you're becoming."* My answer came rather quickly. "Well, Jim, I don't know who I am, and I don't know who I'm becoming either."

That may sound like a strange conversation for two people who had lived together as a married couple for 16 years and had brought four children into the world. What triggered that conversation? The answer sounds like something out of a science fiction movie or a mystery thriller: I was being dramatically changed by *visitations in the night.*

Throughout history, the lives of ordinary people have been forever changed by times of supernatural visitation. When I say visitation, I am referring to those times when "the manifested presence of God comes into our time-space world and invades our unholy comfort zones. He comes to reveal aspects of His personality, His character, His power, and His loveliness, or simply to reveal Himself." Whether these visitations happened to individuals or to large numbers of people in a generation or nation, they always brought about times of *awakening* to the supernatural God.

In his book, *The Lost Art of Intercession*, Jim made two statements that directly refer to supernatural encounters with God in our generation. The first statement came in a chapter where Jim describes what many prophetic people call "refreshing, renewal, and a new level of revival," which is coming to the Church in this generation:

> "We've feasted on the wine of the Spirit and have been refreshed with laughter, joy, and renewal. We have bowed our knees in humility and repentance under the fiery presence of our jealous God, the righteous King of glory. We have been lifted up in His grace as righteous, holy, and pure in His sight. Now, we are about to experience the *wind of God*, characterized by powerful supernatural gifts, supernatural encounters, and angelic intervention!"[1]

Earlier in the same chapter, Jim wrote, "Those of us who are filled with *His* desire and *His* secrets find ourselves launched on a journey of supernatural encounters, intercession, and intervention as we speak forth the decrees of God in the earth by His Spirit!"[2]

Beginning on the Day of Atonement, October 6, 1992, our family entered a nine-week period of supernatural visitations that forever changed our lives—especially mine. In retrospect, I suppose that period was like a compressed "pregnancy" in the spirit measured in weeks instead of months. All I know is that by the time it was over, God had birthed a whole new identity in me that literally changed my relationship with Jim and revolutionized our approach to ministry.

One Incredible Elevator Ride

For nearly two decades, my husband has taught on spiritual growth and the development of spiritual gifts and ministry. He characterizes some people (including himself) as "staircase" people who grow one step at a time and gradually progress toward their destiny in Christ. The second group of people he calls "elevator people" because they seem to suddenly shoot up ten flights of stairs with one major encounter with God. That is what happened to me. One day I was minding my own business trying to muddle along through life, and the next day God showed up and it suddenly was, "Lights, cameras, action!" It was one incredible "elevator ride," and the things that God taught me during my spiritual "pregnancy" motivated me to write this book about encounters with a supernatural God.

I have to tell you that I had no idea that anything was about to happen to me that October night in 1992. All I knew was that I was frazzled and tired. Like millions of other busy parents across the world, I had struggled with my kids during a hard day and I couldn't wait to get them in bed so I could finally get some rest myself. When I say I was "just tired," then I have perfectly described my emotional state in one phrase. I had prayed some of the same prayers you have probably prayed: "Lord, I want to see You. I want to know You. I want to have encounters with You. Help me, God; I just feel too tired and I don't have any energy left." I had no clue just how seriously God took my simple prayer, but He was about to show me.

Though I had walked closely with the Lord from my childhood, I, like many of you, had been struggling to find my own security and ministry in God. One way to put it is that I needed to rediscover personal "ownership" in my relationship with the Lord. Before I met Jim, I had a very strong walk with Jesus, whom I considered to be my best friend. Once Jim and I were engaged and later married, I reacted in the wrong way toward Jim's very strong revelatory gifts and ministry anointing. In other words, I began to unconsciously ride on my husband's spiritual coattails. At times, if I needed to hear from God, I let Jim do the listening for me. Finally, I began to put more trust in what Jim would say the Lord was saying than in my own perception of what He was saying.

As I began to lean more on Jim than on the Lord, the voice of the Holy Spirit gradually became faint to my ears. Then the Lord began convicting me of this imbalance in my life. Tied into this problem was my deep desire to escape the bondage of intimidation and the fear of man. I dreamed of the day when I would be brave enough to step out and take a gamble for God.

That night, I finally put the children to bed and collapsed in bed alone. Jim hadn't made it back from the night class he was teaching at Grace Training Center in Kansas City. Jim told me the next day that during the class, he had mentioned to the students that it was the Day of Atonement. In honor of the spiritual significance of that holy day to the Jews, Jim had led the class in prayers of repentance and dedication, and then he presented them to the Lord. Suddenly, a wind began to blow through the cracks in some of the windows and rattle the Venetian blinds as if in confirmation of their prayers of dedication.

God Is Going to Speak

Class went late that night, and afterward Jim drove home our good friend, Chris Berglund, his teaching assistant at that time. As they were driving, Jim felt his left ear suddenly pop open. He turned to Chris just before our friend got out of the car and said, "Chris, God is going to speak tonight." Jim told me later on, "I had no idea what I was saying, but I knew an encounter was on the way and I guess I automatically assumed that I would be the one who would have the encounter. Little did I know the magnitude and effect of the invasion that was about to come into our lives."

By the time Jim got home shortly after 11:00, I was already asleep in bed. The winds that blew against the windows at the Training Center class also blew in a storm that had grown into a thunderstorm. Jim finally went to sleep around 11:15, but one minute before midnight on the Day of Atonement, Jim woke up instantly and sat up in bed. (His years of prayer and prophetic ministry had conditioned him to look at our digital clock to see what time it was whenever he awakened.)

Earlier that night, our third child, Tyler, had joined me in the bedroom when he was frightened by the storm. When Jim sat up and looked at the clock, little four-year-old Tyler remained sound asleep on the floor by Jim's side of the bed. Jim was startled awake when a lightning bolt crashed down in our backyard, and seemed like it came right through our bedroom window. In the flickering glow of that lightning strike, without warning, Jim suddenly saw a man standing in our room looking straight at him!

This went on for what Jim still calls "the longest minute of my life." A ball of white light came in and hovered like a spotlight over a letter on my dresser. The letter was from David Castro, a prophetic friend from New York City. David had sent us a prophetic word along with some pictures that he had drawn of what he called "an old-fashioned swashbuckler" with a sharp sword. This was a prophetic picture of the authority David felt that God had given us to minister deliverance to those in bondage. The ball of light remained in a fixed position over that letter on my dresser for five hours. This is the way Jim describes his experience that night:

"I was shaking. I mean this was the original 'quake, shake, and bake' time. That room was filled with what I can only describe as 'the terror of God.' I'm not talking about some nice, gentle little fear of God—this was absolutely frightening. It wasn't the first time I'd experienced that kind of terror of God, though. I had encountered it two times before, but each time I knew I was in the holy, manifested presence of God. On this particular night, I felt like I was about to crawl out of my skin.

"This man looked at me, and I looked at him, but neither one of us said anything. When the clock turned to midnight, I heard an audible voice say, 'Watch your wife. I am about to speak to her.' Right after that, the man (I believe he was an angel) disappeared—but the terror of the Lord remained in our room. As soon as the angel disappeared, Michal Ann woke up."

When I woke up that night, I remember that Jim turned to me and whispered, "Ann, an angel has just come." I could feel him trembling, and suddenly I knew why. Jim didn't bother to tell me that his left ear had opened up or that he had told Chris that God was going to speak that night. He didn't even tell me what the angel had said, or what he looked like. (Jim told me later that the angel had the appearance of a man, that he was wearing shoes of some kind and some trousers, and that he was dressed in brown. Jim thought that maybe the angel was a servant messenger of some kind.)

We had been through enough experiences in the past for me to know that when I heard Jim whisper "Ann!" the way he whispered it that night, something major was happening. I immediately thought, *Oh no, it's happening again!* I was really scared, but I also knew that something extraordinarily wonderful was occurring. No one describes the experience better than the venerable Job:

> *Now a thing was secretly brought to me, and my ear received a whisper of it. In thoughts from the visions of the night, when deep sleep falls on men, fear came upon me and trembling, which made all my bones shake. Then a spirit passed before my face; the hair of my flesh stood up!* (Job 4:12-15 AMP)

The terror of the Lord was present the moment I woke up, and no pile of covers was high enough to cover me or shield me from His Presence. I just wanted to crawl to the foot of my bed with about 20 covers over me, but I knew I would still feel as if I was covered by only a thin little sheet. Amazingly, little Tyler slept soundly through the entire ordeal, but Jim and I just shook together under the covers for half an hour. Then Jim did the most amazing thing—he rolled over and fell asleep! I have never been able to understand how he could do that! I thought (between shakes), *How could he leave me alone like that? I thought that at least we were going to go through this together, you know?* No, he went to sleep instead.

I Still Sounded Very, Very Frightened

So there I was, lying awake and shaking in fear under the covers. I thought, *Okay, this is an opportunity from the Lord to be bold, and to go for everything that the Lord has for me.* So I began to cry out to God, "Lord, I want to know what You're doing. I want to hear what You're saying. I invite Your Presence; I invite Your Holy Spirit. Everything that You want to do, I want You to do it. I am just presenting myself here before You." I know I still sounded very, very frightened, but I was putting my best foot forward in the only way I knew how.

The terror of His Presence permeated the room, and I was still shaking, so all I could do was wait and see what the Lord might do. For three days previous I had suffered with severe earaches caused by exposure to the cold weather and wind. My ears were hurting that night, so I was lying on my stomach with one ear on the pillow. Suddenly I began to feel a liquid warmth flow into my exposed ear. It felt like warm oil and it was very soothing. I was being healed.

I was still nearly paralyzed with fear, but I decided to try a big experiment. I really liked how that warm oil felt. So I decided to very carefully and slowly turn my head to see what would happen. Would I cut off the anointing of God and offend Him? I was afraid of making any wrong move that might cause His Presence to leave (even though I was terrified by the experience at the same time).

When I turned my head, the warm oil began to pour into my other ear, and then things suddenly started to change. I had been lying there for about 90 minutes, just waiting on the Lord. I turned to look at the clock and it was 1:34 in the morning. That time was a significant signpost. I didn't know it at that point, but Psalm 134:1 signified what the Lord was going to have me do for the next nine weeks: "Behold, bless the Lord, all servants of the Lord, who serve by night in the house of the Lord!" (Ps. 134:1)

Then I began to feel pressure building up in my head, and it became very intense. I didn't know if I could handle it or not, and I was almost ready to scream. At the very moment when I thought that I couldn't handle it anymore, the pressure moved from my head to my back. It felt like someone had laid a board across my back right along my spine and was trying to literally push the breath out of my body!

I was desperately trying to reach out to Jim, but something was holding my hand back. I felt my body literally being moved away from Jim, while at the same time, this pressure against my back was pressing everything out of me. Then I saw an extreme close-up picture of a horse's eye and I heard the word *horse.* This went on during a period of 30 minutes, which lasted until 2:04 in the morning. I now believe this correlates with this passage in the Book of Proverbs:

> *If you seek [Wisdom] as for silver and search for skillful and godly Wisdom as for hidden treasures, then you will understand the reverent and worshipful fear of the Lord and find the knowledge of [our omniscient] God* (Proverbs 2:4-5 AMP).

I came out of that experience feeling like I didn't even know what I looked like anymore. I actually checked to see if I was still alive by putting my fingers up to my throat to see if I had a pulse. I felt like I had just undergone major internal surgery. Honestly, I was afraid that if I got up and looked in the mirror that my hair would be white or my face would look different. I felt like God had just performed some kind of radical surgery on me, but I didn't know what He'd done.

After this ordeal, Jim and I prayed and asked the Lord to confirm these experiences through our children if they were from the Lord. When little Tyler woke up that morning—without prompting—he stood right up and announced that he had a dream that angels had visited our house. Our oldest son, who was upstairs in bed that night, told us of his detailed dream about a winged white horse!

God Was Trying to Tell Us Something

At 2:04 a.m., Jim suddenly woke up again and asked me what was happening. He could sense that the awesome Presence of the Lord was still in the room. It was already difficult for me to talk, but every time I tried to talk to Jim, I could feel the "waves" of the Presence of the Lord increase even more in their intensity and power. This was most apparent in those moments when I would get too close to the crucial or critical part of my experiences over the past few hours—the fear of the Lord became so great at those times that I just couldn't talk. This left us both shaking in bed. We would rest for 20 minutes in fear and trembling, and when we felt the intensity begin to subside a little bit, we would begin to talk again. Sure enough, each time another wave would come in and engulf us in the room. God was trying to tell us something!

Meanwhile, we noticed that the glowing light was still hovering over my dresser—even though the thunderstorm had passed by and all the lightning was gone! The waves of God's Presence continued to flow over me through the night, and when morning finally arrived, Jim got up and left me in bed. When I finally got up, I was still "jumpy." Every time I came to a corner in a hallway or room of the house, I expected to see an angel there. I was so totally submerged in this supernatural realm that simple things like fixing breakfast were totally beyond me. (It's a good thing this isn't a full-time state of being, or I would be the epitome of the old saying, "You're so heavenly minded that you're no earthly good.") There was no way I could fix my daughters' hair and help my children get ready for school—I just was not operating on a practical plane. I remember sitting on the couch with my face turned away from all the activity going on when one of my children came up behind me and tapped me on the shoulder. I suddenly jumped and looked around as if to say, "Who are you? Oh, you're my son." I was looking for another surprise visitor from the heavenly realm....

That morning I called our intercessory friend, Pat Gastineau, of Atlanta, Georgia. The Holy Spirit had indicated to me that Pat would have discernment on some of the events of the previous night. She shared her perceptions with me, which I found to be quite helpful. Pat interpreted the pressure I experienced on my back as God's tool of driving fear and unbelief out of my life. This seemed to be a picture of what He desires the Church to experience (we'll look at this in later chapters). Thank God for our friends!

I have to say that Jim was very gracious with me, and my kids were very understanding during the next nine weeks. My family got a taste of life without regular "Mom-cooked" meals, and without all the practical things moms do, like cleaning the house.

The very next night, God's Presence again entered our bedroom at about 2:00 in the morning and began to minister to me (while Jim slept on). This pattern was repeated almost every night for about nine weeks. The Presence of the Lord would come so strongly that I would be afraid I might not live through the experience. There were many nights, particularly when Jim was away on a ministry trip, when I would stay up far into the morning hours. I didn't know what I was going to be walking into. I know it sounds strange for someone to link words like *fear* and *terror* with the God of love, grace, and mercy. But we must remember that when God comes to us in intimate communion, He comes to take over. For mortal men and women, that can be a frightening experience. All you have to do is examine all the instances when God or His messengers appeared to mortals in the Scriptures. In virtually every instance, the first thing they said to people was, "Fear not," or "Peace."

Jim began to see a change in me almost immediately. By the time we had our "I don't know who you are" conversation in our kitchen, Jim and I were both being overwhelmed by the magnitude of the changes God had made in me. We had several discussions that included statements like, "Well, Ann, you're not like you used to be—you're not the same person I married." Then I would deliver a very uncharacteristic reply like, "Well, you didn't expect me to stay the same, did you? Didn't you expect me to grow and to change?" So we went back and forth like other real married couples do who are trying to rework and readjust their relationship to accommodate change. We had to reexamine every aspect of how we treated one another. We realized that we had to allow and even encourage each other to come into everything the Lord had for us. That meant we would have to remove every nice little controlling factor, like that statement, "But I like you just the way you were." The proper answer (given in love, of course), was, "Well, honey, if I'm getting closer to God, then you'll like me even more. You can't lose."

Can Two Walk Together?

We discovered that we could no longer assume that we understood what the other one was saying or thinking. We had to step back and become reacquainted. The old, overly familiar statements like, "Oh yeah, I know what you mean," wouldn't do anymore. Once we both realized that God was changing things in our personal walk with Him and in our marriage relationship, we felt the comfort of the Lord. The Bible says, "Can two walk together, except they be agreed?" (Amos 3:3 KJV) We had come into a new place of agreement: Neither one of us knew what I was changing into! As odd as it sounds, it gave us some common ground to work from. We made a commitment to walk with each other *through change*, and this is a huge issue that deals with commitment, covenant, and stretched communication skills. We quickly realized that this has a whole lot to do with the Body of Christ too.

As I prayed about it and talked with other people who were seasoned in the things of God, I began to realize that Jim and I had been exposed to "the jealousy of God." The Lord spoke to Jim about me and said, "Before she was ever yours, she was Mine." That is true for every one of us! Before we ever belonged to anyone else, we were His first, and He will always maintain first rights to us as His beloved. God is jealous for us as His priests and His holy people.

Jim often explains in our meetings, "I actually had to call home to find out what God was saying during those nine weeks, because I was no longer married to this wonderfully sweet woman and mother of our four children—now I was married to an anointed woman of God!" We had to relearn how to relate to one another under these new circumstances. In Jim's words, I was now "possessed by God." He was so cautious that, for a time, he wasn't even sure if it was lawful for him to touch me or not, even though we had already been married for many years! (Remember, this situation only lasted for a relatively short period of time while God was doing a very specific work in me. It wasn't a permanent or long-term situation.)

We began to realize that we were not what we once were, and we were not yet who we were going to become. We had to learn how to walk with one another in grace and mercy. In retrospect, I think our kitchen talk that night in November of 1992 was one of the most wonderful things that ever happened to us! It helped us come into another place of agreement concerning the will of God for our lives and the need for us to drop our old limitations and stereotypes. Jim summed it up when he said, "We had entered into another level of wisdom and understanding. It was an adventure, I have to admit. I mean, this was one of the most fun times we had ever had in our lives. It scared the living daylights out of us, but it was a tremendous time."

The Church is beginning to experience exactly what Jim and I experienced in our marriage. Before the angelic visitations, I partially buried my gifts and abilities under Jim's considerable giftings. There are countless branches of the Church who desperately need the hidden and silent gifts that have been buried in the congregation. They have been silent for too long, while the stronger and more visible gifts have been accepted for a long time. They're used to being the "mouthpieces" of God, the decision-makers and shakers of the Kingdom. The problem is that change is in the wind. God is raising up the quiet giftings, the hidden resources He planted in His Church long ago. That means that there is going to be tension in the household of God for a while. The old tried and true leaders in the Church will face an incredible challenge to yield and to give and take as God moves these new gifts into visible ministry. Does it mean that God plans to do away with the existing leaders and ministries in the Church today? Absolutely not. But it does mean that God wants a full-voiced choir declaring His purposes instead of a program exclusively devoted to soloists. He wants to see duets, trios, quartets, ensembles, instrumentalists, and more!

Change Is Coming

As believers in the one Body of Christ, we all need to learn how to listen to each other. We need to take a step back and let those rise to speak whom God has anointed for specific times and places. If we begin to walk in Spirit-led discernment, then we will realize where the anointing is by watching the Spirit. I think the anointing of God in this generation is going to come from some places that we would never expect or guess carried God's anointing and fire.

Change is coming to the Church. The nine weeks of angelic visitations came to our home years before the Holy Spirit brought the Father's blessing to a small fellowship in Toronto, Ontario, or before He descended in power on Brownsville Assembly of God Church in Pensacola, Florida. Today, we realize that the Lord was giving us a peek into the future of the Church through those visitations. Our experience was a precursor of what He wants to do with His Bride, the Body of Christ.

God is determined to see every gift and deposit that He has planted in His family rise up and bear good fruit. In many cases, change in His Church and an impact on the lost is coming through encounters with a supernatural God. Are you ready for visitations in the night?

Lord, give me the grace to embrace change. Come and make me into the person You desire me to be. Invade my unholy comfort zones with visitations of Your Presence. In Jesus' name, amen.

Endnotes

1. Jim W. Goll, *The Lost Art of Intercession* (Shippensburg, PA: Destiny Image Publishers, 1997), 119.

2. Goll, *The Lost Art of Intercession,* 107.

Chapter 2

Supernatural Encounters and the Angels of God

Jim W. Goll

And suddenly an angel of the Lord appeared [standing beside him], and a light shone in the place where he was. And the angel gently smote Peter on the side and awakened him, saying, Get up quickly! And the chains fell off his hands (Acts 12:7 AMP).

It should be no surprise that our supernatural God would bring change to our lives and ministries through supernatural means. One of the most prominent of these supernatural means are angels. Contrary to popular belief, angels are not merely the stuff of old wives' tales, cute Bible stories for children, or prime time television shows.

According to the Bible, there are specific orders and characteristics of angels. Billy Graham says that "angels belong to a uniquely different dimension of creation which we, limited to the natural order, can scarcely comprehend."[1] Theologian C. Fred

Dickason remarks that there "is enough evidence to say that there are distinct and graded ranks, but not enough evidence to make a complete comparison or organizational chart."[2] I want to quickly and briefly lay a solid Bible-based foundation for the nature and work of angels before we go any further in our discussion of supernatural encounters.

Archangels: The Covering Cherubs

First of all, it is clear that there are three or more different ranks or types of angels, and there are many different types of authority given to angels. This authority seems to vary according to the type of angelic assignment. The English term, *archangel* appears in both the Old and New Testaments. It refers to "covering or chief angels," and they have other angels of lesser rank and authority under their command. The apostle Paul linked an archangel with the second coming of Christ, writing, "For the Lord Himself will descend from heaven with a shout, with the voice of the *archangel*, and with the trumpet of God..." (1 Thess. 4:16). The Book of Jude tells us that the *archangel Michael* disputed with the devil over Moses' body (Jude 9), and he is referred to in Revelation 12:7. The term *covering cherub* also appears in Ezekiel 28. Three archangels are mentioned by name in the Scriptures, and each of these created beings seems to possess unique qualities and realms of authority.

Lucifer: The Archangel Who Fell Through Pride

Lucifer is the archangel who was ejected from Heaven and given another name, satan. The name *lucifer* (meaning "son of the morning") appears only once in the Scriptures (see Is. 14:12 KJV). After his ejection from Heaven, he was called *satan* (a Hebrew term meaning "the adversary"). Three key passages in the Bible describe lucifer's fall from Heaven through pride and rebellion. They also provide invaluable insights into the nature and characteristics of archangels in general (see Is. 14; Ezek. 28; Rev. 12). Jesus Himself provided a fourth witness to satan's fall when He said, "I was watching Satan fall from heaven like lightning" (Lk. 10:18).

How you are fallen from heaven, O Lucifer, son of the morning! How you are cut down to the ground, you who weakened the nations! (Isaiah 14:12 NKJ)

You were in Eden, the garden of God; every precious stone was your covering: the ruby, the topaz, and the diamond; the beryl, the onyx, and the jasper; the lapis lazuli, the turquoise, and the emerald; and the gold, the workmanship of your settings and sockets, was in you. On the day that you were created they were prepared. You were the anointed cherub who covers... (Ezekiel 28:13-14).

And another sign appeared in heaven: and behold, a great red dragon having seven heads and ten horns, and on his heads were seven diadems. And his tail swept away a third of the stars of heaven, and threw them to the earth. And the dragon stood before the woman who was about to give birth, so that when she gave birth he might devour her child. ... And there was war in heaven, Michael and his angels waging war with the dragon. And the dragon and his angels waged war, and they were not strong enough, and there was no longer a place found for them in heaven. And the great dragon was thrown down, the serpent of old who is called the devil and Satan, who deceives the whole world; he was thrown down to the earth, and his angels were thrown down with him (Revelation 12:3-4,7-9).

Satan was an anointed and beautiful covering cherub with a professional understanding of music and worship. When he fell from Heaven, he was dispatched "like lightning," according to Jesus. This fallen covering cherub is also referred to as the "red dragon" who swept away a third of the stars, or angels of Heaven, in his rebellious scheme before he was quickly ejected.

Gabriel: The Messenger Archangel

The archangel Gabriel is mentioned five times in the Bible. The Old Testament prophet Daniel mentions his name three times, and then Gabriel appears twice in the Gospel of Luke. Every time this archangel is mentioned, he brings a specific message from the

Presence of the Lord, which is why he has often been called the "messenger angel." However, Daniel's record also reveals that Gabriel too is involved in cosmic warfare alongside the archangel Michael. Very often you see the unique phrase, "the man Gabriel," referring to his manlike appearance.

> *...standing before me was **one who looked like a man**. And I heard the voice of a man between the banks of Ulai, and he called out and said, "Gabriel, give this man an understanding of the vision." So he came near to where I was standing, and when he came I was frightened and fell on my face; but he said to me, "Son of man, understand that the vision pertains to the time of the end." Now while he was talking with me, I sank into a deep sleep with my face to the ground; but he touched me and made me stand upright. And he said, "Behold, I am going to let you know what will occur at the final period of the indignation, for it pertains to the appointed time of the end"* (Daniel 8:15-19).

> *...while I was speaking in prayer, **the man Gabriel**, whom I had seen in the vision at the beginning, **being caused to fly swiftly**, reached me about the time of the evening offering. And he informed me, and talked with me, and said, "O Daniel, I have now come forth to give you skill to understand. **At the beginning of your supplications the command went out**, and I have come to tell you, for you are greatly beloved; therefore consider the matter, and understand the vision"* (Daniel 9:21-23 NKJ).

> *Suddenly, a hand touched me, which made me tremble on my knees and on the palms of my hands. And he* [Gabriel] *said to me, "O Daniel, man greatly beloved, understand the words that I speak to you, and stand upright, for **I have now been sent to you**." While he was speaking this word to me, I stood trembling. Then he said to me, "Do not fear, Daniel, for **from the first day** that you set your heart to understand, and to humble yourself before your God, **your words were heard**; and I have come because of your*

*words. But **the prince of the kingdom of Persia withstood me twenty-one days; and behold, Michael, one of the chief princes, came to help me**, for I had been left alone there with the kings of Persia"* (Daniel 10:10-13 NKJ).

And the angel answered and said to him, "I am Gabriel, who stands in the presence of God; and I have been sent to speak to you, and to bring you this good news (Luke 1:19, addressed to Zechariah).

Now in the sixth month the angel Gabriel was sent from God to a city in Galilee, called Nazareth, to a virgin engaged to a man whose name was Joseph, of the descendants of David; and the virgin's name was Mary (Luke 1:26-27).

Michael the Warring Archangel

One of the most prominent archangels in the Scriptures is Michael, the chief prince specifically mentioned four times by name in the Scriptures. One passage in the Book of Daniel describes the interaction and cooperation between the two archangels, Gabriel and Michael, along with the latter's special assignment from God:

...Michael, one of the chief princes, came to help me... (Daniel 10:13).

*...Yet there is no one who stands firmly with me against these forces except **Michael your prince*** (Daniel 10:21).

*But **Michael the archangel**, when he **disputed with the devil** and argued about the body of Moses, did not dare pronounce against him a railing judgment, but said, "The Lord rebuke you"* (Jude 9).

*And there was war in heaven, **Michael and his angels** waging war with the dragon. And the dragon and his angels waged war, and they were not strong enough, and there was no longer a place found for them in heaven. **And the great dragon was thrown down**, the serpent of old who is called the devil and Satan, who deceives the whole world; he was thrown down to the earth, and his angels were thrown down with him* (Revelation 12:7-9).

Michael has been given a certain jurisdiction or a place of rule that deals with the destiny of Israel and the Jewish people. He is the guardian and prince over Israel, and he seems to play the most prominent role in matters of warfare and the forceful execution of God's commands. The fact that Michael was involved in a dispute with satan over Moses' body tells us that angels also have something to do with the resurrection of the dead.

Cherubim and Seraphim

There are two types of angels specifically mentioned and described in the Scriptures. The *cherub* (the "im" added to the end of the word makes it plural) is nearly always referred to as a "covering cherub." The Bible passages referring to lucifer (now called satan) during his days of obedience plainly called him a "covering cherub." Gabriel and Michael also appear to be covering cherubs. The first mention of a cherub is in Genesis 3:24:

> *So He drove the man out, and at the east of the garden of Eden He stationed the **cherubim**, and the flaming sword which turned every direction, to guard the way to the tree of life* (Genesis 3:24).

Genesis 3:24 tells us that when God drove Adam and Eve out of the Garden of Eden, He stationed *cherubim* at the gate to guard the way to the tree of life. When God told Moses to build the ark of the covenant, He also gave detailed instructions about the two covering cherubs made of gold positioned on each side of the mercy seat. The specific language is very interesting:

> *And you shall make **two cherubim** of gold, make them of hammered work at the two ends of the mercy seat. And make one cherub at one end and one cherub at the other end; you shall make the cherubim of one piece with the mercy seat at its two ends. And the cherubim shall have their wings spread upward, covering the mercy seat with their wings and facing one another; the **faces of the cherubim are to be turned toward the mercy seat**. ... And there I will meet with you; and from above the mercy seat, from between the two cherubim which are upon the ark of the testimony, I will speak to you*

about all that I will give you in commandment for the sons of Israel (Exodus 25:18-20,22).

God always speaks to us in the place of His mercy because our performance will always fall short. This place of mercy is between the wings of the covering cherubs. It is a place of reverence, awe, and the fear of the Lord.

And He [God Almighty] *rode upon a **cherub**, and did fly: and He was seen upon the wings of the wind* (2 Samuel 22:11 KJV).

The Seraphim

Seraphs, or seraphim, are only mentioned twice in the Bible, and both mentions appear in Isaiah 6. Here the prophet is describing his vision of the Lord on the throne, which he received after King Uzziah's death:

> **Seraphim** *stood above Him, each having six wings; with two he covered his face, and with two he covered his feet, and with two he flew. And one called out to another and said, "Holy, Holy, Holy, is the Lord of hosts, the whole earth is full of His glory." And the foundations of the thresholds trembled at the voice of him who called out, while the temple was filling with smoke. Then I said, "Woe is me, for I am ruined! Because I am a man of unclean lips, and I live among a people of unclean lips; for my eyes have seen the King, the Lord of hosts." Then **one of the seraphim** flew to me, with a burning coal in his hand which he had taken from the altar with tongs. And he touched my mouth with it and said, "Behold, this has touched your lips; and your iniquity is taken away, and your sin is forgiven"* (Isaiah 6:2-7).

The seraphim in Isaiah's vision had six sets of wings, which is significantly different from the two wings attributed to cherubs. With two wings the seraphim covered their faces, showing the attribute of worship and humility. With two other wings they covered their feet, perhaps revealing their place of servanthood. The final pair of wings were used to fly. These angels may be similar to the "four living beasts" with six wings described in Revelation 4:6-10. These beings never rest, but day and night, they cry out, "Holy, holy, holy is the Lord God, the Almighty." I believe that the seraphim are a very distinct category of angels, although the Scriptures do not give us any specifics other than those provided by the prophet Isaiah. They release a particular cry of worship, and their voices are so powerful that they can shake the earth or compel great leaders to bow before the Lord in humility. They carried the coals of fire that released a power of sanctification to the life and ministry of Isaiah.

Other Biblical Categories of Angels

The Bible gives us a number of additional insights into angels through descriptions of their duties, appearance, or deeds. *Guardian angels* are referred to in Matthew 18:10 with regard to little children, although the actual term never appears in Scripture. These angels "continually behold the face of God," and there is no evidence that these angels are reassigned as children grow up into adulthood.

The first chapter of the Book of Ezekiel describes *four living beasts* dispatched from Heaven in a great cloud filled with flashing fire. They seemed to move at the speed of light to accomplish their assignments. They glowed with a hot heat like "burnished bronze" and each one had four sets of wings. As in the description in Revelation, these beasts each had four faces: that of a man in the front, of a lion on the right, of a bull on the left, and of an eagle to the rear. One verse is especially interesting: "And each went straight forward; wherever the spirit was about to go, they would go, without turning as they went" (Ezek. 1:12). These four living beasts described by Ezekiel bear an obvious resemblance to the seraphim described by John in the Book of Revelation, differing only in the number of wings the beings possessed. In any case, these "living beasts" or seraphim seem to only go wherever the Spirit is going.

The apostle John also refers to a *strong angel* in Revelation 5:2: "And I saw a strong angel proclaiming with a loud voice, 'Who is worthy to open the book and to break its seals?' " Something must have stood out about this angel that led John to describe it by inspiration of the Spirit as a "strong angel." This is also implied in Revelation 18:1, where John writes, "After these things I saw another angel coming down from heaven, *having great authority*, and the earth was illumined with his glory." Whether this was an archangel or one of the four living creatures, I don't know. But it is clear that there are different ranks and categories of angels. The Book of Revelation also speaks of angels assigned to specific church bodies in cities such as Philadelphia, Laodicea, Pergamum, or Sardis (see Rev. 1). In my opinion, I think that the Lord may have assigned angels to carry or help release the Word of God into different cities and regions. Possibly this portrays a "territorialism" of certain angels.

Isaiah spoke of *"the angel of His presence"* in Isaiah 63:9, saying, "In all their affliction He was afflicted, and the angel of His presence saved them; in His love and in His mercy He redeemed them; and He lifted them and carried them all the days of old." Basilea Schlink remarks, "The angels of God are bright and shining beings, emanating light and mirroring the glory of God."[3] I am convinced that angels are used to release the manifested Presence of God. When they show up, the atmosphere changes! But I don't know whether this term is referring to a particular category of angels or to "the angel of the Lord," which we will cover next.

God told Moses in the Book of Exodus:

Behold, I am going to send an angel before you to guard you along the way, and to bring you into the place which I have prepared. Be on your guard before him and obey his voice; do not be rebellious toward him, for he will not pardon your transgression, since My name is in him. But if you will truly obey his voice and do all that I say, then I will be an enemy to your enemies and an adversary to your adversaries. For My angel will go before you and bring you in... (Exodus 23:20-23).

The term *angel of the Lord* appears 56 times in 52 verses in the Old Testament. In many of these cases, there is something or Someone at work who is greater in authority and magnitude than the angels we've studied so far. It is generally accepted that these are "theophanies," or visible appearances of the Lord Jesus Christ before His incarnation as a human being. The Second Person of the Godhead could appear in the form of an angel before His "birth" as a human being in Bethlehem. Many scholars feel that the "fourth man" who appeared with the three Hebrew children in the midst of the flames in the fiery furnace of the King of Babylon was actually a theophany (see Dan. 3:25). Abram probably experienced a theophany in Genesis 18 when three angelic visitors came to him. One of the three may well have been Jesus Christ in a form that appeared to be an angel.

Characteristics of Angels

1. The *language forms* of angels include a heavenly language unknown to natural man (see 1 Cor. 13:1), and earthly dialects known to man. They can speak softly or shout loud enough to shake the earth, and all angels, great and small, sing praises to God and before man.

2. Certain angels have *wings*. Some have two wings, some have four wings, and some have six wings.

3. Some angels appear to be dressed in *white garments*. The angel or angels who rolled away the stone from the Lord's tomb had appearances that were "like lightning" (see Mt. 28:2-4); and "two men in white clothing" appeared to the disciples who were staring into the sky after Christ ascended (see Acts 1:9-11).

4. Angels play *musical instruments*. Revelation chapter 8 speaks of seven angels with trumpets (see also 1 Thess. 4:16). Angels use trumpets to announce God's will or warn people of eternal judgment.

5. Angels often have the *appearance of men*. Two angels of judgment met Lot in Sodom in Genesis 19. Their

appearance was so pleasing that the homosexuals in the city wanted to rape them—before they were struck blind by the angels. Hebrews 13:2 warns us to be hospitable, for we might entertain angels unaware. Why? Because angels can take on the appearance of men in their look, walk, talk, and culture.

6. Angels can come as *wind or fire* (see Heb. 1:7; Ps. 104:4).

The opposite of worshiping angels is the denial of their existence. According to Acts 23:8, the party of the Sadduccees claimed that there was no resurrection, nor angels, nor spirit. The chief religious leader of Israel in the time of Jesus and Paul was a Sadducee. God doesn't want us to become Sadducees. On the other hand, the Pharisees acknowledged the existence of all three of the things the Sadducees denied, but they didn't believe it in a personal way. These men believed that they existed, but they didn't believe they could *know* and experience the resurrection, the Spirit, the angelic realm, or the supernatural ways of God.

One passage in Second Kings 6 illustrates seven key points we need to remember about angels:

Now when the attendant of the man of God had risen early and gone out, behold, an army with horses and chariots was circling the city. And his servant said to him, "Alas, my master! What shall we do?" So he answered, "Do not fear, for those who are with us are more than those who are with them." Then Elisha prayed and said, "O Lord, I pray, open his eyes that he may see." And the Lord opened the servant's eyes, and he saw; and behold, the mountain was full of horses and chariots of fire all around Elisha (2 Kings 6:15-17).

This passage illustrates seven key points to remember about angels and angelic activity:

1. They may be present and unperceived at any time.

2. They may be present and unseen, but perceived by feeling or hearing (I urge you to read Ezekiel 10:5).

3. They may be visible to one person and invisible to another person standing right next to the first.

4. You may pray that someone's eyes may be opened to this revelatory angelic realm.

5. You can grow in spiritual sensitivity.

6. You will be astonished when you finally see into the angelic realm.

7. Reality will eventually come to your heart: "For those who are with us are more than those who are with them" (2 Kings 6:16b).

The Ministry and Function of Angels

Among the 300 Scriptures about angels in the Bible, we find three primary warnings concerning angelic beings:

1. *We are not to worship angels.* "Let no man beguile you of your reward in a voluntary humility and worshipping of angels..." (Col. 2:18 KJV).

2. *We are not to revile angels.* "Yet in the same manner these men, also by dreaming, defile the flesh, and reject authority, and revile angelic majesties" (Jude 8). (See also Second Peter 2:10-11.)

3. *Judge every message, whether from men or angels.* "But even though we, or an angel from heaven, should preach to you a gospel contrary to that which we have preached to you, let him be accursed" (Gal. 1:8).

There are also three primary functions of angels, although we will examine 14 specific angelic functions in this chapter. The three primary functions are:

1. *Service to God.* "Praise Him, all His angels; praise Him, all His hosts!" (Ps. 148:2) Angels are created beings, and God is the Creator. The first function of every angel is Godward.

2. *Service to Christians.* "And of the angels He says, 'WHO MAKES HIS ANGELS WINDS, AND HIS MINISTERS A FLAME OF FIRE.' ... Are they not all ministering spirits, sent out to render service for the sake of those who will inherit salvation?" (Heb. 1:7,14) We are the created beings who inherit salvation.

3. *Performance of God's Word.* "Bless the Lord, you His angels, mighty in strength, who perform His word, obeying the voice of His word! Bless the Lord, all you His hosts, you who serve Him, doing His will" (Ps. 103:20-21). There appear to be two or three different ways this works. The first involves the direct command of God, such as when God commanded Gabriel to deliver a message to Mary in the Gospel of Luke. The second involves the dispatch of angels in answer to intercessory prayer. This happened when Daniel interceded for Israel and Gabriel was sent to him (see Dan. 10:11-12). The third may well involve the release of angelic activity in response to *our* utterance of God's *rhema* word to us in certain situations. Angels will not obey man's word, but they may well obey God's Word through man as we echo God's Word or voice in the earth by His Spirit.

Specific Examples of Angelic Ministry

"Angels are ministers and dispensers of the divine bounty toward us. Accordingly, we are told how they watch for our safety, undertake our defense, direct our path, and take heed that no evil befall us."[4] There are at least 14 ministries attributable to angels in God's Word:

1. *Angels minister in the Presence of God.* Isaiah mentions the "angel of His presence" (probably a theophany of Jesus Christ) who would save and preserve (see Is. 63:9). Such an angel illuminated the earth with His glory in Revelation 18:1.

It is recorded that in Charles Finney's evangelistic meetings, an encampment of angels would come to a spot about a mile away from his meeting site. He felt that the angels were used to help release the Presence of God. Our friend, Pastor Jim Croft, was counseling two women in his church office in Florida. As he began to pray for them, he saw two winged angels standing behind the women. The angels appeared to flap their wings and, when they did, Jim saw something like a golden aura released into the room. This released the Presence of God and both women began to rest in the Spirit right in their chairs as the touch of God came upon them.

2. *Angels bring God's Word.* God sent angels to tell Joseph about Mary's pregnancy and to warn him to take Mary and Jesus to Egypt (see Mt. 1:20; 2:13,19). Angels appeared to Zacharias and then Mary (see Lk. 1:19,26-27). They also delivered a resurrection proclamation (see Mt. 28:1-7).

3. *Angels release dreams, revelation, and understanding.* The angel Gabriel released understanding to Daniel concerning the endtimes (see Dan. 8:15-19). Revelation 1:1 specifically says that God "communicated it [the revelation] by His angel to his bond-servant John."

4. *Angels give guidance and direction.* An angel of the Lord told Philip to meet the Ethiopian eunuch in Acts 8:26. In the Old Testament, it was an angel who guided Abraham's servant in his search for a wife for Isaac (see Gen. 24:7). Paul reassured the frightened men in his ship that no one would die in the storm because "...this very night an angel of the God to whom I belong and whom I serve stood before me, saying, 'Do not be afraid, Paul...' " (Acts 27:23-24).

5. *Angels bring deliverance.* One angel killed 185,000 Assyrians who threatened God's people (see Is. 37:36;

2 Kings 19:35). Billy Graham writes in his book, *Angels: God's Secret Agents*:

"In the early days of World Word II Britain's air force saved it from invasion and defeat. In her book, *Tell No Man*, Adela Rogers St. John describes a strange aspect of that weeks-long air war. Her information comes from a celebration held some months after the war, honoring Air Chief Marshall Lord Hugh Dowding. The King, the Prime Minister, and scores of dignitaries were there. In his remarks, the Air Chief Marshall recounted the story of his legendary conflict where his pitifully small complement of men rarely slept, and their planes never stopped flying. He told about airmen on a mission who, having been hit, were either incapacitated or dead. Yet their planes kept flying and fighting; in fact, on occasion pilots in other planes would see a figure still operating the controls. What was the explanation? The Air Chief Marshall said he believed angels had actually flown some of the planes whose pilots sat dead in their cockpits."[5]

6. *Angels provide protection*. They guard little children, have charge over and protect believers, and "camp" around the saints and deliver those who fear God (see Mt. 18:10; Ps. 34:7; 91;11-12). Billy Graham also shared a true story from the experiences of the late Corrie ten Boom in the Ravensbruck Nazi concentration camp:

"Together we entered the terrifying building. At a table were women who took away all our possessions. Everyone had to undress completely and then go to a room where her hair was checked.

"I asked the woman who was busy checking the possessions of the new arrivals if I might use the toilet. She pointed to a door, and I discovered that the convenience was nothing more than a hole in the shower-room floor. Betsie stayed close beside me all the time. Suddenly I had an inspiration [Now how did she get the inspiration I wonder?], 'Quick, take off your woolen underwear,' I whispered to her. I rolled it up with mine and laid the bundle in a corner with my little Bible. The spot was alive with cockroaches, but I didn't worry about that. I felt wonderfully relieved and happy. 'The Lord is busy answering our prayers, Betsie,' I whispered. 'We shall not have to make the sacrifice of all our clothes.'

"We hurried back to the row of women waiting to be undressed. A little later, after we had had our showers and put on our shirts and shabby dresses, I hid the roll of underwear and my Bible under my dress. It did bulge out obviously through my dress; but I prayed, 'Lord, cause now thine angels to surround me; and let them not be transparent today, for the guards must not see me.' I felt perfectly at ease. Calmly I passed the guards. Everyone was checked, from the front, the sides, the back. Not a bulge escaped the eyes of the guard. The woman just in front of me had hidden a woolen vest under her dress; it was taken from her. They let me pass, for they did not see me. Betsie, right behind me, was searched.

"But outside awaited another danger. On each side of the door were women who looked everyone over for a second time. They felt over the body of each one who passed. I knew they would not see me, for the angels were still surrounding me. I was not even surprised when they passed me by; but within me rose the jubilant cry, 'O Lord, if thou dost so answer prayer, I can face even Ravensbruck unafraid.' "[6]

7. *Angels minister upon the death of the saints.* Psalm 116:15 says, "Precious in the sight of the Lord is the death of His godly ones." According to Jude 9, Michael the archangel personally disputed with the devil over the body of Moses (and obviously had his way). According to Luke 16:22, angels carried the body of the poor man named Lazarus to "Abraham's bosom" when he died. Many witnesses have said that their eyes were opened at the death of loved ones, and they saw them carried away by angels. Billy Graham notes in his book, *Angels: God's Secret Agents,* "…in that last moment…He will have His angels gather you in their arms to carry you gloriously, wonderfully into heaven."[7]

8. *Angels impart strength.* Angels were sent to minister strength to Jesus after His 40-day fast and temptation in the wilderness (see Mt. 4:11). The same thing happened in the Garden of Gethsemane (see Lk. 22:43). Daniel was also strengthened by an angel in Daniel 10:16.

9. *Angels release God's healing.* An "angel of the Lord" stirred the water in the pool of Bethesda in John chapter 5, and the first person to touch the waters was healed. The prophetic evangelist William Branham said an angel imparted the gifts of healing to him during an angelic visitation on May 7, 1946.

10. *Angels minister to God through praise and worship.* An angelic chorus sang "Glory to God in the highest" when they pronounced the birth of Jesus (see Lk. 2:14). The Book of Revelation describes scenes of "ten thousand times ten thousand" angels declaring, "Worthy is the Lamb" (Rev. 5:11-12 KJV).

11. *Angels conduct war.* Jacob encountered an army of angels (see Gen. 32:1-2). Michael and his angels defeated satan and his princes in open combat in the heavenlies (the princes in Daniel 10:13, and satan and all his angels in

Revelation 12:7). There is a strong indication that the high praises of God in our mouths become supernatural weapons of warfare in the hands of angels to bind "...their kings with chains, and their nobles with fetters of iron" (see Ps. 149:5-8).

12. *Angels serve as divine watchers.* They look after the historical affairs of mankind and are quick to notice and respond to sins of man against God (see Dan. 4:13,17). "And immediately the angel of the Lord smote him [King Herod] because he gave not God the glory: and he was eaten of worms, and gave up the ghost" (Acts 12:23 KJV).

13. *Angels release God's judgments.* Angels struck the Sodomites with blindness and killed nearly 200,000 Assyrians (see Gen. 19:11; 2 Kings 19:35). They brought death to stubborn Egypt and struck down Herod for blasphemy (see Ex. 12:21-23; Acts 12:23). And at the end they will execute the final judgments of God on the earth and its rebellious inhabitants (see Rev. 16:17).

14. *Angels are God's reapers and gatherers.* They are sent to preach the gospel and to reap the endtime harvest (see Rev. 14:6,14-19). Angels will gather the lawless and the elect for their appropriate reward (see Mt. 13:39-42; 24:31).

Unemployed Angels?

As a final note in this chapter, you should know that the angels of Heaven appear to be grouped into military-style contingents, only on a much larger scale than any human equivalent. Even one angel is sufficient to destroy the most powerful contingent of armed men in any age or century, but very often they go into battle in groups. Two or more angels teamed up to carry Lazarus to Paradise in honor according to Jesus in Luke 16:22. The Lord said He could summon 12 legions of angels to His aid at any time in Matthew 26:53. (A Roman legion was a military unit of

4,000 to 6,000 soldiers. That means Jesus had more than 70,000 angels instantly available to Him at any time.)

The total number of angels is probably beyond human counting. The Book of Revelation refers to "ten thousand times ten thousand, and thousands of thousands" of angels (Rev. 5:11 KJV). This is a "Hebrewism" or Hebrew idiom meaning "innumerable." It describes a scene containing far more angels than even the first figure of speech could convey. This term is also echoed by Daniel (see Dan. 7:10 KJV). Hebrews 12:22 (KJV) describes "an innumerable company of angels" in heavenly Jerusalem, and Deuteronomy 33:2 (NIV) tells us that the Lord "...came with myriads of holy ones from the south...." Dr. Gary Kinnaman, in his excellent book, *Angels Dark and Light*, states this:

> "We can only guess how many angels there may be. Some people have tried to guess exactly. Fourteenth-century mystics arrived at a precise figure—301,655,722—by employing elaborate but obscure calculation. Wild speculations like this governed the theological studies during the middle centuries. Some of the early Lutherans, in a work called *Theatrium Diablolrum*, estimated that there were 2.5 billion devils, a number later raised to 10,000 billion!"[8] I don't know how many angels there are, but I think there are enough available to do all the things God wants to see accomplished in our lives and generation. I often say, "I have a suspicion that some of these angels are unemployed. They are waiting for the call to be released through our intercession. I think it is time for us to learn how to walk with God and tap into all the heavenly resources He has made available to us."

> *Lord, open the eyes of my heart that I might truly know, "Greater are they who are with us than they who are in the world." Send forth the angels of protection to watch out over me. Send forth Your messengers with the word of the Lord. I welcome Heaven's arsenal to wage war in my behalf. Thank You, Lord, for Your care and plan for me. In Christ's name I pray. Amen.*

Endnotes

1. Billy Graham, *Angels: God's Secret Agents* (Garden City: New York: Doubleday, 1975), 18.

2. C. Fred Dickason, *Angels: Elect and Evil* (Chicago: Moody Press, 1975), 18-19.

3. Basilea Schlink, *The Unseen World of Angels and Demons* (Old Tappan, New Jersey: Fleming Revell, 1985), 81.

4. John Calvin, *Calvin's Institute* (Grand Rapids, Michigan: Associated Publishers, n.d.).

5. Graham, *Angels*, 163-164.

6. Graham, *Angels*, 90-91.

7. Graham, *Angels*, 155.

8. Dr. Gary Kinnaman, *Angels Dark and Light* (Ann Arbor, Michigan: Servant Publications, 1994), 40.

Chapter 3

How Do You Hear God's Voice?

Michal Ann Goll

The sheep that are My own hear and are listening to My voice; and I know them, and they follow Me (John 10:27 AMP).

I was desperate to hear God's voice. An important conference in another state was looming on the horizon, and I was a scheduled speaker along with Jim. I was praying on the run, asking the Lord, "What do You have for these people?" I barely had any time to sit down and read my Bible, let alone develop a "deep" message to transform lives.

I'm not a famous speaker on the Christian speaking circuits—I'm a certified, full-time, mostly stay-at-home mother of four growing children and administrator of our ministry; plus I'm married to Jim Goll, a man who travels nationally and internationally as part of our ministry. Time is an endangered and scarce resource for me—yet I had to hear God's voice. I knew that when I stood up before the people at that conference, excuses wouldn't do. They all had those kinds of problems. They had invested their time and money in that conference for *answers*. (And I surely didn't have any from my own self for them. I was in prime position for a miracle.)

Night after night, I would go to bed and say, "Lord, what do You have for these people?" I was hoping that He would speak to me in my dreams. (Sometimes that's one of the best times He can speak to me, because it is just about the only time my head is disengaged from the responsibilities of daily life.) This dry period of frustration seemed to drag on week after week for more than a month.

Just two weeks before the conference was scheduled to begin, I had a dream in which I saw Jim posing this question to a number of people in a meeting in a classroom: "How do you hear the Holy Spirit?" I immediately felt my heart leap within me, and I started waving my hand while saying, "I know. Let me tell them. I know how to hear the Holy Spirit." (Now remember, this was in a dream.) Jim said, "I have to leave for a few minutes, and I'll be back." He started to walk out, but then he saw me waving my hand in the back and said, "Oh yeah, Ann, you can answer that question. Come on up here and tell them."

That was when I woke up, feeling like an electric or magnetic energy was flowing over my body. I've discovered that I usually feel like that whenever the Lord has dispatched angels to give me messages in the night. I felt that way after my dream of the classroom, and I knew that God had deposited something in me.

I woke up from this dream and heard the song based on Philippians 4:8, which says, in effect, "Whatsoever things are true, whatsoever things are honest, whatsoever things are just, whatsoever things are pure, whatsoever things are lovely, and of a good report. If there be any virtue, if there be any praise, think on these things." This song went through my mind over and over, even though I hadn't sung it for years.

Then I thought of the little instrument called a tuning fork, and of the unique purpose it serves. I feel that the Lord is planting a tuning fork in each of our lives. It is a fixed measure and starting point where He wants us to begin all our days and symphonic movements as individuals vitally joined in one spiritual body. Why a tuning fork? Think of its primary use—each time it is struck, it produces a sound of unvarying pitch. It sets the standard of true pitch by which all other instruments calibrate themselves for accuracy and perfect blending of musical tones.

For years now, Jim has been conducting "Fire on the Altar" intercessory training conferences in the U.S. and abroad (I help out when I can). He has been handing out questionnaires to intercessors and church leaders in all those places for years, and one of the most commonly asked questions we have seen is this: "*How do you discern the voice of the Holy Spirit?*"

Time to Tune In

The Lord has shown me that one of the keys to accurately discerning the voice of the Holy Spirit is found in the Holy Ghost tuning fork in Philippians 4:8. Every time you strike it, it will produce vibrations and tone of an unvarying pitch. That's the way we need to be. As we think on the good things, the true things, the things that are honest, pure, lovely, and of a good report, *it tunes our heart* to the very heart pitch of God.

According to the Merriam-Webster Dictionary, you "tune" something "to bring into harmony; to adjust for precise functioning; to make more precise, intense, or effective."[1] I don't know what you feel about this, but there is something in me that wants to be in harmony with the Creator of the universe! I want Him to adjust me all that He wants to so I will function with precision, intensity, and effectiveness!

We all need to "tune in," but most of us treat it as a one-time necessity. The fact is that we need to constantly fine-tune our spirits to the heart of the Lord. Have you ever felt like God had changed His "broadcast channel" on you? Being human and the creatures of habit that we are, we tend to get used to always hearing God in the same way. We act like He's not supposed to change His methods. When we realize that our "receiving set" just isn't working anymore, we point our finger at the Broadcaster, not at the receiver. "I am just not hearing God like I used to. *I don't understand what He's doing.* I just don't understand what He's saying anymore. I am not hearing Him."

Sometimes I think God is shaking His head at our inflexibility and saying, "Okay, I'm going to stretch you a little bit. I think it's time to change the channel. I know you hear Me very well on 'Channel 4' in the clean atmosphere of a worship service. Let me switch My beam of anointing to another channel that requires an inquiring heart boosted with tenacity in the middle of a day cluttered with confusion, discomfort, and chronic fatigue. Let's see if you can make that adjustment." This sometimes painful process of "tuning in" and focusing on the Lord, regardless of circumstance or personal emotional state, is vital to our growth in Christ.

What to Tune Out

There is another side to this "tuning" process. High fidelity radio and precision radar systems not only lock in on desired frequencies, but they also tune out extraneous noise or "ground clutter." In the same way, we not only need to develop and exercise our ability to tune in to God's voice at all times, but we also need to tune out the distractions and interruptions that so effectively block out or mask God's still small voice. This "fine-tuning" process isn't a rapid one. It is a lifelong process that constantly builds the character and heart of God into our lives. We need to learn how to "tune out" all of the voices of criticism, doubt and unbelief, negativity, gossip, and rumors that bombard us every single day! This is serious business.

Take That First Step

One of the most vital ingredients in our relationships with our mechanic, our pastor, and our personal physician is *honesty*. They can't help us if they don't have the honest facts about our condition or need. It is even more important for us to be honest with ourselves and with the Lord. The first step in any "tune-up" is an *honest evaluation*. God will examine you to see what work needs to be done, and you don't have to worry that He will be shocked by any of your revelations. He won't stomp off if you tell Him that you're upset, or that you're disappointed, or burned out, or even angry. It won't surprise Him one bit because He already knows about it. (He's just waiting for you to tell Him.) I'm not talking about having a "gripe session" and chewing out God—although I confess I've shared some of those with Him too. He just patiently listened until I ran out of steam. Then He began to release a little trickle of His oil of anointing in my heart to bring me healing and grace. That's when I would say, "God, I am angry, and I don't want to be this way. Will You help me?"

God wants us to be real and honest so He can clean out our spiritual "pipeline." We get so busy sometimes that we don't even know how much junk is clogging our lifeline to Jesus. *Don't be afraid to be honest with the Lord.* Be completely honest with Him. Cultivate thankfulness and gratefulness. God wants to establish grateful hearts full of thanksgiving in us.

When you get angry with God, take time to sit down and ask yourself, "Okay, what is good? What are the things that God has done for me?" It may be difficult at first, because we tend to get very wrapped up in ourselves during our "down times." Don't give in. Make the decision to turn away from ungodliness and openly confess to God, "Okay, Lord, I know I've been mad, and I'm upset. But I choose by my will to think on the good things that You've done for me." This releases the power of God in your heart to clean you out. It disarms the anger and frustration, and eases pain. It helps you step out of your own limited place of frustration and into God's spacious place of grace and loving acceptance. Honesty frees you to become heavenly and eternity minded. I love what the Bible says in Hebrews 12:

Therefore then, since we are surrounded by so great a cloud of witnesses [who have borne testimony to the Truth], let us strip off and throw aside every encumbrance (unnecessary weight) and that sin which so readily (deftly and cleverly) clings to and entangles us, and let us run with patient endurance and steady and active persistence the appointed course of the race that is set before us, looking away [from all that will distract] to Jesus, Who is the Leader and the Source of our faith [giving the first incentive for our belief] and is also its Finisher [bringing it to maturity and perfection]. He, for the joy [of obtaining the

prize] that was set before Him, endured the cross, despis-
ing and ignoring the shame, and is now seated at the right
hand of the throne of God. Just think of Him Who endured
from sinners such grievous opposition and bitter hostility
against Himself [reckon up and consider it all in compari-
son with your trials], so that you may not grow weary or
exhausted, losing heart and relaxing and fainting in your
minds. You have not yet struggled and fought agonizingly
against sin, nor have you yet resisted and withstood to the
point of pouring out your [own] blood (Hebrew 12:1-4
AMP).

During a difficult period of time, I was having a struggle with
anger. When God showed me this Scripture passage, it totally disarmed me. God was saying, "You have not yet endured hardship
to this degree. Don't grow weary, don't faint, be strong." You can
gain courage and strength from understanding and seeing the
hardship that Jesus bore. We can be encouraged by observing the
grace that God extends to other believers as they walk through trials and embrace the cross. You can gain strength by thinking of
Him. Just think of Him.

Do You Need a Tune-up?

In a world filled with obstacles, resistance, controversy, and
occasional sorrows, each of us is bound to come to a point when
our daily efforts to tune in just aren't enough to bring us into harmony with the heart of God. When we suffer a major blow or drop
to the ground, we often are "knocked out of adjustment" so seriously that we need some heavy-duty maintenance and tune-up
work. Everywhere Jim and I go, we find lovely believers who are
suffering from significant pain that may stem from early childhood abuse or injury, from unresolved grief after the death of a
loved one, or from an area of unforgiveness that has progressed to
deep-seated bitterness. Many times these deep wounds and major
shocks don't yield to "self-help efforts." That is why God placed
us in a *body* of believers and gave us supernatural grace gifts.
Some of us may need a "lube" job, some of us may need our

"timing" adjusted, and others of us need a major overhaul of our internal working parts so our engines can work properly.

I don't know what we're going to become, and I don't know what's down the road, *but God does*. I believe that His Holy Spirit wants to move and have free reign in us. We may think that we are on the cutting edge of faith now, but if we yield to the Spirit of God, the lives of adventure that we have in Him today will seem infantile compared to those in the days to come. If we allow God to tune us up, if we learn how to tune in to His most tender whisper, if we learn how to tune out every distraction, then I think we will discover what life can be like in the atmosphere of radical faith and relationship with the King of the universe.

Tuned for Tomorrow's Journey

God wants to bring totally new definitions to things that we haven't even contemplated before. You and I may be thinking today, *Well, my engine feels pretty good. It's running pretty good too.* The problem is that we don't know what is down the road a few miles or days from now. We don't know what race God has assigned us to. We don't know when it's going to take place, or where. We have no idea what obstacles will try to block our path to the finish line. We don't know when we are going to come to a sharp snake turn, or when we will need new pads on our brakes to keep us from losing control on a mountain road or to help us avoid a collision. We *all* need a few tune-ups from time to time—not just for today, but for tomorrow as well. The only one who can give us a tune-up is the original Manufacturer, although He often uses His factory-trained mechanics in the Body of Christ to do the job.

In all situations, we are tuned to the one great tune of the universe: Jesus Christ. Every aspect of Paul's admonition in Philippians 4:8 (KJV) is focused on the pride and joy of the Father: "...whatsoever things are true, whatsoever things are honest, whatsoever things are just, whatsoever things are pure, whatsoever things are lovely, whatsoever things are of good report, if there be any virtue, and if there be any praise, think on these things." Can you think of anything more lovely than Jesus Himself? Is there anything more pure, is there any person more pure, or more lovely than Jesus Himself? Is there anyone who has been more faithful, is there anyone who has been more gracious, more forgiving?

The Parable of the Seed That Is Sown

Years ago, the Lord set me on a path of instruction and began to teach me how to train my thoughts. I'm still on that path. Along the way, the Lord led me to the parable of the sower of the seed in chapter 8 of the Gospel of Luke. As I read the first verse which says, "The sower went out to sow his seed..." (Lk. 8:5), I felt like I was reading the passage for the first time. It brought encouragement to me as the thought came to mind, *The Lord is sowing His seed. It's not an issue of whether or not He wants to, or if He will. God's Word says He is sowing His seed, the Word of God.* The Lord is sowing His seed and it is falling on us even as you read these words...

> *"The sower went out to sow his seed; and as he sowed, some fell beside the road; and it was trampled under foot, and the birds of the air ate it up. And other seed fell on rocky soil, and as soon as it grew up, it withered away, because it had no moisture. And other seed fell among the thorns; and the thorns grew up with it, and choked it out. And other seed fell into the good soil, and grew up, and produced a crop a hundred times as great." As He said these things, He would call out, "He who has ears to hear, let him hear"* (Luke 8:5-8).

Jesus explains to the disciples in Luke 8:11 that "the seed" in His parable is the Word of God. When I read that Scripture, I realized that I had always considered this verse as a "salvation" passage that referred to lost people hearing the gospel. The Lord refocused my understanding to see that He is continually sowing His Word in us, planting direction and guidance in our lives. I want you to read the Lord's own interpretation of His parable in the Amplified Version of the Bible:

Those along the traveled road are the people who have heard; then the devil comes and carries away the message out of their hearts, that they may not believe (acknowledge Me as their Savior and devote themselves to Me) and be saved [here and hereafter]. And those upon the rock [are the people] who, when they hear [the Word], receive and welcome it with joy; but these have no root. They believe for a while, and in time of trial and temptation fall away (withdraw and stand aloof). And as for what fell among the thorns, these are [the people] who hear, but as they go on their way they are choked and suffocated with the anxieties and cares and riches and pleasures of life, and their fruit does not ripen (come to maturity and perfection). But as for that [seed] in the good soil, these are [the people] who, hearing the Word, hold it fast in a just (noble, virtuous) and worthy heart, and steadily bring forth fruit with patience. No one after he has lighted a lamp covers it with a vessel or puts it under a [dining table] couch; but he puts it on a lampstand, that those who come in may see the light. For there is nothing hidden that shall not be disclosed, nor anything secret that shall not be known and come out into the open. Be careful therefore how you listen. For to him who has [spiritual knowledge] will more be given; and from him who does not have [spiritual knowledge], even what he thinks and guesses and supposes that he has will be taken away (Luke 8:12-18 AMP).

There is a difference between hearing and listening. Hearing merely requires the physical ability to detect sound, but listening requires the involvement of the mind in the natural realm, and of the heart in the spiritual realm. I believe that is why Jesus said again and again, "He who has ears to hear, let him hear." Virtually everyone around Him had the physical ability to hear—that wasn't what He was talking about. Only a few "had ears to hear," meaning only a few had the *desire to listen* and receive what He said. It's time for the Church to be "all ears"! When we, like Dumbo, are all ears, we will really take off and fly!

Listen From the Heart

You can *hear* and ignore, but it is impossible to ignore a thing and *listen* to it at the same time. Listening to the voice of the Lord is an attitude and action of the heart. You poise your heart in such a way that, whatever you're doing, you are always trying to hear the Lord. You wait in a positive, or even in an aggressive, posture. It means you have a certain confidence that God is going to speak, and you have tuned your ear to hear His slightest whisper. God's voice can come suddenly at times, but if you "have ears to hear," then you may be busy going about your daily activities and duties and His voice will hit your ear with such power that it almost takes your breath away or jars you out of your automatic mode. At other times, you will barely hear a gentle whispering in the wind in a still small voice, yet it will bypass your ears and sink deep into your spirit, confirming what you already know in your heart—God is talking to you once again. In the words of Eliphaz the Temanite, "Now a word was brought to me stealthily, and my ear received a whisper of it" (Job 4:12). Very often, the Holy Spirit will speak so softly that He gives you just enough to prompt the question, "What was that? Was that You, Lord?"

Once Jim asked our dear friend, evangelist Mahesh Chavda, an important question. He asked, "Now that you have walked with the Lord all these years, fasted for 40 days on many occasions, and seen many great healings and miracles through your life, how does the voice of the Holy Spirit come to you?" Mahesh responded just the way Jim was afraid he would: "Oh, you must understand. The closer I get to Him, the gentler His voice becomes." We must learn to listen.

God knows what He's doing, and one of the things He is teaching us is how to posture ourselves for a lifestyle of listening. We don't want to miss a single whisper from His beloved lips! So be careful how you listen. It can make all the difference in your life in Christ. Listen to the good and ignore the bad, as David wrote in the Psalms, speaking prophetically of Jesus Christ: "Thou hast loved righteousness, and hated wickedness; therefore God, Thy God, has anointed Thee with the oil of joy above Thy fellows" (Ps. 45:7). Be careful how you listen and what you listen to.

I found it difficult to hear the Lord in those weeks before the conference because I was dealing with so many anxieties and cares. Jim was away ministering in England and Germany, and I had the kids almost around the clock. Meanwhile, I was also dealing with the daily ministry affairs and some very difficult relationship situations. My heart and mind slipped out of focus as I became so caught up in all the turmoil, cares, and anxieties of my daily existence.

When I finally had an hour to myself one night, I just sat there and said, "Jesus, Jesus." It wasn't fancy, but in that place of just calling on His name, all my cares just seemed to melt away. The fog lifted and I saw in a moment of time how carried away I had been. I was amazed at how quickly things became clear when I said His name. (Just say "Jesus" right now and let His Presence soak down into your spirit.)

Obstacles and Assurances About Hearing From God

Everyone has times when he or she just can't seem to hear from God. It can help if you know that other people have to deal with this problem and why these dry times come to all of us. Sometimes they come because we've begun to doubt that God really speaks to us today, or because we haven't really made a strong commitment to Jesus Christ as Lord of our lives. Some of us go through dry times because we are hiding unconfessed sin or living a "double standard" lifestyle. (The solution in these cases is obvious.)

At other times, we are unaware of the scriptural evidence proving our right and privilege to hear from God personally. A lack of teaching on how to pursue such a listening prayer experience can make things even worse. A few of us have to battle secret fears of being called a "religious fanatic" or "mentally ill," and others are afraid of opening themselves up to the "wrong spirits" or being led astray by the enemy. There is a better way.

You Can Have Assurance That God Is Speaking

If you can say, "Yes!" to these statements, then you can rest assured *that God is speaking to you*!

1. What I heard helps me to respect the Lord with a godly fear, and to depart from evil (see Job 28:28).

2. The message I received from God increases my faith in His Word, as well as my knowledge and understanding of it (see Prov. 4:7).

3. When I obey the things God told me to do, they produce in my life one or more of the spiritual fruits of purity, peace, gentleness, mercy, courtesy, good deeds, and sincerity without hypocrisy (see Jas. 3:17).

4. What I heard strengthens me "with all power" so that I can keep going no matter what happens (see Col. 1:11).

5. It causes me to experience joyfulness and thanksgiving to the Father (see Col. 1:12).

Loren Cunningham, founder and director of Youth With a Mission, has been accurately receiving God's direction for many years. He has taught hundreds, if not thousands, of people how to hear from God. Many if not most of these people were "non-professionals" who nonetheless wanted to hear from God and do His work in the mission fields. YWAM has trained and sent out teenagers, housewives, carpenters, accountants, former drug addicts, single parents, retired couples, and recovered alcoholics into the mission fields, with miraculous results. I think that he has something to share for you and me as well. In his book, *Is That Really You God?*, Loren offers "12 points to remember" when hearing the voice of God, which I've condensed and summarized:

1. *Don't make guidance complicated.* It's hard *not* to hear God if you really want to please and obey Him! Follow three simple steps that will help you hear His voice:

   a. *Submit* to His lordship. Ask Him to help you silence your own thoughts, desires, and opinions of others. You want to hear only the thoughts of the Lord (see Prov. 3:5-6).

b. *Resist* the enemy, use the authority Jesus Christ has given you to silence the voice of the enemy (see Jas. 4:7; Eph. 6:10-20).

c. *Expect* an answer. Ask the question that is on your mind, but then *wait* for Him to answer. Expect your loving heavenly Father to speak and He will (see Jn. 10:27; Ps. 69:13; Ex. 33:11).

2. *Allow God to speak to you in the way He chooses.* Don't tell Him how to guide you. Listen with a yielded heart and you will hear. He may choose to speak to you through:

   a. *His Word.*

   b. *An audible voice.*

   c. *Dreams and visions.*

   d. *The quiet inner voice.* This is probably the most common of all the means (see Is. 30:21).

3. *Confess any unforgiven sin.* A clean heart is a prerequisite to hearing God (see Ps. 66:18).

4. *Ask yourself, "Have I obeyed the last thing God told me to do?"*

5. *Get your own leading.* God will use others to *confirm* your guidance, but you should also hear from Him directly (see 1 Kings 13).

6. *Don't talk about your guidance until God gives you permission to do so.* The main purpose of waiting is to help you avoid four pitfalls: pride, presumption, missing God's timing and method, and bringing confusion to others.

7. *God will often use two or more spiritually sensitive people to confirm what He is telling you* (see 2 Cor. 13:1).

8. *Beware of counterfeits. Satan has a counterfeit for every-thing of God that it is possible for him to copy* (see Acts 8:9-11).

9. *Opposition of man is sometimes guidance from God* (see Acts 21:10-12). The important thing to remember here, again, is to remain *yielded* to the Lord. Rebellion is never of God.

10. *Every follower of Jesus has a unique ministry* (see 1 Cor. 12; 1 Pet. 4:10-11). The more you seek to hear God's voice *in detail*, the more effective you will be in your own calling.

11. *Practice hearing God's voice and it will become easier.* It's like picking up the phone and recognizing the voice of your friend: You know his or her voice because you've heard it so much.

12. *Relationship is the most important reason for hearing the voice of God.* If you don't communicate, then you don't have a personal relationship with Him. True guidance comes from getting closer to the Guide. We grow to know the Lord better as He speaks to us. As we listen to Him and obey, we make His heart glad (see Ex. 33:11; Mt. 7:24-27).

I Walked With God in My Dreams

One of the ways God speaks to us today is through our dreams. We will look at this in much greater detail in a later chapter, but I want to tell you how God taught me an important lesson about His love through a dream. (I encourage you to write down a summary of any dreams you have.) There will be seasons when God will speak to you on certain subjects through your dreams. If you record them, you will be able to review them as you progress in your walk in Christ and so gain greater understanding into their meaning or purpose.

I had a dream in which I would take walks with an older gentleman, and I remember that those times were very sweet and pure. I remember that we were standing together and facing each other one time, and I knew that He just longed for me in the purest sense. (I suppose it was similar to how a good father or mother just feels their heart break every time they see their beautiful daughter or son playing and laughing.) I knew in the dream that He loved the fragrance of my hair, and it was like He was just waiting to embrace me. I could almost hear Him say, "Will you please let Me hug you because I can't wait to smell the fragrance of your hair." It really baffled me, and I thought, *You like the fragrance of my hair?* I could almost hear His soft answer, "Yes, I do. I love it. I love it very much, and I can't take in your fragrance enough."

My heavenly Father wanted me to understand that this is the kind of love He has for every one of us. These things are so unimaginable to us that our first reaction is to think, *Oh, surely not.* His reply is persistent and passionate, "Oh yes, I love every part of you. I love every aspect of your being, I love you, and I love to be with you." In one meeting, Jim received a prophetic song from the Lord that said, "Don't you know that there's a pain in My heart whenever I am separated from you in any way whatsoever." I felt a pain in my heart the moment Jim started to sing, and there just wasn't anything else I could do other than feel the pain of God over our separation from Him. God's love for us is so great that it hurts Him when He can't totally embrace us. He wants to so encompass us and wrap us up in Himself that we become one. I don't know how it works, but I know it's true.

Silence Is Golden

The old saying goes, "Silence is golden." It is so true. Quieting our soul before the Lord tunes us in to His golden Presence. We must learn these almost forgotten ways in a fast-paced society.

You may be someone who finds silence quite natural, or you may enjoy being on your own, but not everyone finds it so easy to be alone. Many people face quite a struggle when they are alone. If that's the case with you, don't give up. You're not a failure. If you are spending time alone and in silence for the first time, then you need to understand something. If you've been running from inner fears or insecurities for a long time, and you try to sit down and silence yourself, you will *still be running* for a while. It will probably take a while for your inner man to slow down and get quiet. Give yourself time. Many people use their activity and busyness to help them avoid the deeper questions and concerns of life. The problem is, most of us are cluttered inside with the accumulations of years of hopes and fears, plans and ideas, and light and darkness. The Holy Spirit first of all has to clear a space before He can settle down and begin His wonderful work of healing and restoration.

Beware of Impatience and Hastiness

The Lord gave me a burden for this book because He wants to do some healing in the lives of many who will read these words (and that may well include you). I believe that the Lord is pursuing the coming generation, and He has a very strong anointing that He wants to impart to them. At the same time, the enemy is trying to bring an unreasonable impatience and hastiness to the older generation of this society, which could well doom their ability to influence the younger generation for good and godliness.

God's will in the affair is already on record. He declared through His prophet that in the last days, He would turn the hearts of the fathers to the children, and the hearts of the children to the fathers (see Lk. 1:17). We need to intercede and be on guard for our children. We need to ask God to give us grace as parents and mentors so we won't feed into that spirit of the world that says, "hurry, hurry, hurry." We are so oriented to a fast food mentality. We need to change our approach and realize that we are in this for the long haul and allow God to prepare a full, seven-course meal.

As we learn to slow down to take time to meditate on the Lord, to come into union with Christ, then old issues, old memories, can begin to float to the surface. With them sometimes come pain, disappointment, and grief, perhaps over words spoken or deeds done in haste or anger. The enemy wants those old issues to remain so they can act as roadblocks to keep us from knowing and experiencing the love of God to the fullest measure.

Healing the Hurts That Hinder the Flow

Multitudes of people have experienced crippling hurts and wounds in this day. I don't care how old you are, or whether your mother and father are alive or not; the Lord wants to heal every hurt and wound you carry in your heart and mind. The Father wants to put His healing balm on your heart. Whether you've been on the receiving end or the giving end of hurt, God's love is available to you. Perhaps you feel like you've missed it with your kids by being too harsh or insensitive toward them. The point is simply this: There is grace, love, and forgiveness waiting for you in God's hand.

You may not realize it, but when the Father's love sweeps over you, it will often uncover a lot of hidden things that have been imprisoning you in secret bondage, such as unconfessed and concealed sin or hurt. Many times, after there has been a release of the Spirit in this way, the enemy brings up all kinds of questions to bring dissension between people. The cure is simple and effective: "Whatsoever things are true, and honest, and of a good report, if there be any virtue, or any praise, think on these things."

We must graft in the good Word of God into our soul to cleanse, heal, restore, and save us. We must do this in order to tune our hearts to hear His voice. These simple points of listening, slowing down, quieting our soul, and ingrafting the Word of God are all essential if we are to cooperate with the process of healing the hurts that hinder the flow of hearing God's voice.

Receiving Revelation

Now let me state some of the most important points we need to know about personally receiving revelation from God. I've taken these points and historical examples from Jim's teaching on "Receiving Revelation."

We have to realize that God *wants* us to be a people of revelation! We don't have to beg Him for it because He wants it more than we do. He passionately wants to light the "lamp of revelation" in our hearts (see 1 Sam. 3:1-3; 2 Kings 6:17; Dan. 12:3; Jn. 16:13-15). The first step is for us to simply ask!

We need to believe that Peter was *talking about us* when he stood up in Jerusalem on the Day of Pentecost and quoted the prophecy of Joel. He was talking about you and me when he said "sons and daughters" would prophesy, and young men would see visions, old men would dream dreams, and men and women would prophesy (see Acts 2:17-18). According to Peter, dreams, visions, and revelation are *scriptural*, they are for *you*, and they are for *today*. Our job is to ask and receive according to James 4:2 and John 16:24. Do you want the spirit of wisdom and revelation? Then ask!

How does revelation come? It comes in answer to prayer (see 1 Kings 3:3-5; Dan. 2:17-19), in special situations (see Gen. 28:10-12; Mt. 2:19), and in response to fasting (see Dan. 9-10). God has commanded each of us to "set our minds and affections on things above," or on the things of Heaven and our Father (see Rom. 8:5-9; 12:1-2; Col. 3:1-2).

Once again, I must emphasize that *quietness is the "incubation cradle" for revelation*. God makes it clear that quietness is one of the necessities of receiving revelation from Him. He will not compete for our attention; He *demands* our total attention (see Ps. 46:10; 131:1-3; Is. 30:15). We must be cradled in His love, which casts out fear, and lean our head on His heart. Quietness is a great key to unlocking the spirit of revelation in your life.

Learn From Those Who Have Heard His Voice

We can learn from the wisdom of those who have successfully and consistently heard from God in their lives. You can always pick these people out from the crowd because their lives bear the fruit of God's Presence and anointing. Here are some excerpts from the writings and journals of some of these people:

Henri Nouwen (1930s)[2]

A spiritual life without discipline is impossible. Discipline is the other side of discipleship. The practice of a spiritual discipline makes us more sensitive to the small, gentle voice of God.

The prophet Elijah did not encounter God in the mighty wind or in the earthquake or in the fire, but in the small voice

(1 Kings 19:9-13). Through the practice of a spiritual discipline we become attentive to that small voice and willing to respond when we hear it.

It is clear that we are usually surrounded by so much outer noise that it is hard to truly hear our God when He is speaking to us. We have often become deaf, unable to know when God calls us and unable to understand in which direction He calls us.

Thus our lives have become absurd. In the word *absurd* we find the Latin word *surdus*, which means "deaf." A spiritual life requires discipline because we need to learn to listen to God, who constantly speaks but whom we seldom hear.

Jesus' life was a life of obedience. The word *obedient* comes from the Latin word *audire*, which means "listening." Jesus was always listening to the Father, always attentive to His voice, always alert for His directions. Jesus was "all ear." That is true of prayer: being all ear for God. The core of all prayer is indeed listening, obediently standing in the presence of God.

Without solitude it is virtually impossible to live a spiritual life. Solitude begins with a time and a place for God, and Him alone. Jesus says, "…Go into your room, and when you have shut your door, pray to your Father who is in the secret place…" (Mt. 6:6 NKJ).

Thomas Kelly (1893–1941)[3]

Mister Eckhart wrote, "As thou art in church or all, that some frame of mind carry out into the world; into its turmoil's and fitfulness." Deep within us all there is an amazing inner sanctuary of the soul, a holy place, a Divine Center, a speaking Voice, to which we may continuously return. Eternity is at our hearts, pressing upon our time-torn lives, warning us with the intimations of an astounding destiny, calling us home unto Itself.

It is a light which illuminates the face of God and casts shadows and new glories upon our faces. It is seed stirring to life if we do not choke it. It is Shekinah of the soul, the presence in the midst. Here is the slumbering Christ, stirring to be awakened, to become the soul we clothe in earthly form and action and He is within us all.

Mental habits of inward orientation must be established. An inner, secret turning to God can be made fairly steady after weeks and months and years of practice and lapses and failures and returns. It is as simple as Brother Lawrence found it, but it may be long before we can achieve any steadiness in the process.

Begin now as you read these words, as you sit in your chair, to offer your whole selves, utterly and in joyful abandon, in quiet, glad surrender to Him who is within. In secret ejaculations of praise, turn in humble wonder to the Light, faint though it may be. Keep contact with the outer world of sense and meanings. Behind the scenes, keep up the life of simple prayer and inward worship. Let inward prayer be your last act before you fall asleep and the first act when you awake.

Madame Guyon (1648–1717)[4]

In "beholding the Lord" you can come to the Lord in a totally different way.

The mind has a very strong tendency to stray away from the Lord. Therefore, as you come before the Lord to sit in His presence, beholding Him, make use of the scripture to *quiet* your mind. The way you do this is really quite simple. First read a passage of Scripture. Once you sense the Lord's presence, the content of what you have read is no longer important. The scripture has served its purpose; it has quieted you mind; it has brought you to Him.

Next, while you are before the Lord, begin to read some portion of scripture. As you read, *pause*. The pause should be quite gentle. You have paused so that you may set your mind on the Spirit. You have set your mind *inwardly*—on Christ.

While you are before the Lord, hold your heart in His presence. Yes, by faith you can hold your heart in the Lord's presence. Now, waiting before Him, turn all your attention toward your spirit. The Lord is found *only* within your spirit, in the recesses of your being, in the Holy of Holies; this is where He dwells.

Needed: Grace to Take the Practical Steps

If these men and women were able to cultivate an intimate lifestyle of continuous communion with God, then so can you. God is not a "respecter" of persons; He loves and responds to each one of us the same way—with great joy and delight. For our part, we need to take some very practical steps to make sure we don't hinder the flow of pure revelation from God's heart into our own.

We need to walk in the Spirit of God and live godly lives. The Bible compares the lives of those who don't follow God to the waters of a troubled sea that is always kicking up dirt and debris (see Is. 57:20-21). We need to guard our hearts and make sure that worries do not dominate our thinking and our actions. The solution is to cast all our cares upon Jesus, because He cares for us (see Ps. 37:8; 1 Pet. 5:7). The same is true of anger, lust, bitterness (from unforgiveness), and addictions of any kind (see Eph. 4:26; Rom. 13:10-14; Heb. 12:15; Eph. 5:18, respectively). This special attention to our lifestyle even extends to our choices for entertainment and how much of it we seek (see Mk. 4:24). It also helps to maintain a consistent schedule of prayer, meditation, work, and play in your life. But the most important and effective thing you can do to hear God's voice is to *ask Him to speak*!

We also must each realize something very elementary and important: God likes to speak to His kids! How do we hear? We hear because of His great grace set toward us. We hear because He speaks loud and well enough for us to catch it. We hear because He pursues us. He wants us to hear His voice more than we want to hear it!

Isaiah 50:4-5 explains it this way:

[The Servant of God says] The Lord God has given Me the tongue of a disciple and of one who is taught, that I should

know how to speak a word in season to him who is weary. He wakens Me morning by morning, He wakens My ear to hear as a disciple [as one who is taught]. The Lord God has opened My ear, and I have not been rebellious or turned backward (Isaiah 50:4-5 AMP).

The Lord will open your ear. He will awaken the interest of your heart to enable you to listen. He will come to you morning after morning, night after night, and pursue you with His great love. How do you hear God's voice? He helps you!

Pray this prayer right now before you move on to the next chapter or do anything else:

Heavenly Father, tune my heart to hear Your voice. Enroll me in Your school of the Spirit. Teach me how to quiet the noise of my soul in order to hear Your voice, that I might follow You. Help me to realize that You want me to hear Your voice more than I want to hear it. Help me to receive the spirit of revelation. For Your glory's sake, I make this request in Jesus' name. Amen.

Endnotes

1. *Merriam-Webster's Collegiate Dictionary*, 10th ed. (Springfield, Massachusetts: Merriam-Webster, Inc., 1994), **tune** (v), 1272.

2. Richard Foster and James Bryan Smith, *Devotional Classics* (San Francisco: Harper Collins Publishers, 1993), 95.

3. Foster and Smith, *Devotional Classics*, 205-206.

4. Foster and Smith, *Devotional Classics*, 321-322.

Chapter 4

No More Fear!

Michal Ann Goll

For God did not give us a spirit of timidity (of cowardice, of craven and cringing and fawning fear), but [He has given us a spirit] of power and of love and of calm and well-balanced mind and discipline and self-control (2 Timothy 1:7 AMP).

Several years ago, Jim and I were conducting a church retreat in Nashville, Tennessee (long before we moved to that area from Kansas City). All weekend long, I was pondering my ongoing battle with intimidation. I had set my heart on being free from every form of intimidation, but I was still in the "waiting mode."

On Sunday morning I perceived that nearly everyone attending the meeting was feeling like he or she didn't have a place to function in his or her giftings and callings. The people felt like some kind of "spiritual bottleneck" was hindering the flow of the Spirit in their lives and was therefore exerting control over them. They wanted to freely breathe the air of God's Spirit, but they felt like there was just a tiny little neck through which the refreshing breath of the Spirit could come through, and everyone was crowding up to this tiny opening inside this "bottle." I felt a tremendous burden from the Lord for them, and was crying out to Him on their behalf.

Then two dear friends belonging to a prayer group from Atlanta, Georgia, came over to me and said, "Can we pray for you?" I said, "Yes," and we moved into a little side room. These ladies immediately began to come against the spirit of intimidation they sensed was oppressing me, and I began to release an involuntary scream that was quite loud. (It had to be involuntary because I would have never done something like that on my own.) Someone from the worship service in the adjacent room came to the door and said everyone over there had quieted down and were beginning to serve communion. They politely told us, "You're making too much noise. You've got to be quiet."

I wanted to be sensitive to what was going on out there, but at the same time, I knew that if I quenched what the Spirit was doing in me, I wouldn't get free and my old enemy, intimidation, would have the upper hand once again. I felt like the Lord was saying, "How badly do you want to be set free from this thing? Are you willing to endure criticism as a cost for freedom, if necessary?" My decision was quick and resolute. I wanted freedom, and from deep within me, the cry for freedom came forth—and it was loud! As this loud cry came out of my mouth, I literally felt something that I have never felt before or since. I felt something come out of the top of my head. I could feel its dimensions inside my head— it was shaped like a railroad spike—and was much the same size. I could actually feel this thing lift out of my head, and then I felt what I could only call "an empty space" in my head where the spike had previously been. (You can imagine what kind of comments that can generate from the quick-witted.) I knew something wonderful had just happened, and somehow God had answered years of prayers!

We finished the conference, and eventually everybody went home. Jim and I had already decided to stay over at this retreat center for one more night just to have some time alone. Meanwhile, I was still in my contemplative mode, trying to figure out what God had done with me and where I was to go from there.

When things quieted down I shared what had happened with Jim. As far as Jim was concerned, the meetings were over and he was finally enjoying some time with me. So he was in a kind of slap-happy, silly mood that afternoon as we went out for a walk together side by side. Jim began to clap his hands and swing his arms extra wide—just wide enough to pop me on the shoulder each time. Obviously he was teasing and flirting with me, which was great, but I wasn't in any mood to be hit on the shoulder at that moment. To me, Jim was "invading my personal private space." I tried to be nice and I said, "Jim, please don't do that."

Okay, Hit Me!

Jim was determined to be feisty and he said with that patented "innocent" look, "Do what?" (as his hand once again popped me lightly on the shoulder).

"Jim, please don't hit me," I said, this time with more firmness. But it was too late. Jim had too much momentum to stop. "Hey, I'm not hitting you" (and he kept popping me on the shoulder). I appealed to him again, very graciously, of course. That was when he turned to me, pulled up his shirt sleeve, and said, "Okay, hit me."

Without thinking or rationalizing, I watched my fist double up, saw it draw back, and *Pow!* saw it hit right on his arm. Both of us reacted with the same amount of shock. My mouth dropped open, and I thought, *What did I just do? I just hit my husband! I can't believe it!* I mean, I've never hit anybody in my life, except when I was a child. Jim's mouth dropped open, and he stared at his shoulder and started rubbing it with his other hand. Then he looked at me with an expression that said it all. He didn't even have to say what he was thinking—it was all over his face: *You really did it! I can't believe it!*

In that instant God showed both of us that the very thing those ladies had prayed over me had come to pass. I truly was delivered from intimidation. (Please understand that I'm not advocating that wives hit their husbands. Jim really didn't mind getting hit in the shoulder, honestly. In fact, he gets a lot of mileage out of the story in his seminars by working up every little detail he can. He tells people how I curled up my fingers, balled them into a rock-hard fist, pulled my arm back—demonstrated in true dramatic fashion—and then released a bone-bruising blow, punctuated by a loud "whoop." We do have fun!)

The Lord showed us in that little incident just what He had accomplished in me that day. We both just started laughing and talking back and forth, "Look what you did!" "I know, look what I did! Isn't this bizarre?" I was overjoyed and free at last, and in this case, God's answer to my prayer came through the effectual fervent prayer of my anointed intercessor friends. Their prayer provoked a supernatural encounter between the Spirit of God and the foul spirit that had been oppressing me and dogging my thoughts for years. As I was interceding for that group of believers for the very same need, God heard my cry and sent dear friends to intervene on my behalf at that very moment so that I could be set free.

During that supernatural encounter in prayer, God removed the "stronghold" or strangling grip that the spirit of intimidation had held over my life since childhood. That doesn't mean that I don't still struggle with it from time to time, because I do. It is just that it comes as an average temptation now instead of a recurring monster that I've feared. I am very conscious of intimidation, and I've made up my mind in Christ never to knuckle under to its fear again.

A Vision to Wear

A few years later, I was scheduled to speak at a "Women in the Prophetic" conference in Kansas City. I had been carrying this conference in my heart for months, bathing it in prayer. I was to address the subject of overcoming intimidation. I knew that in order to minister on this issue, I had to face the enemy of intimidation, only this time it wasn't just for me personally; I had to fight that enemy for the 2,000 women who would be in attendance. I had to be victorious, not in myself, but in the Lord! I could not let one ounce of fear stand in the way of freedom for these dear ones. I had to walk up on the platform as bold as a lion. But I felt like David, small and insignificant, sent to kill a mighty giant called intimidation. So I was crying out to God! He would have to blow on my little stones in my sling. The night before my scheduled session, God gave me a short, but very strategic, prayer, "God, let me do this with *no fear!*" When I prayed that prayer, I saw a T-shirt that had the words, *No Fear*, displayed across the front. I thought, *Oh, wouldn't that be good? Thank You, Lord! I will go into this session with this vision of NO FEAR written across my heart!*

The first session was about to start in a couple of hours. Jim was at home that weekend caring for our children. I told him of my experience, and he said, "You've got to go buy a 'No Fear' T-shirt for your session." I told him that I didn't have time to find one, and Jim replied, "I'll go find you a T-shirt!" So while I was at the conference, Jim went shopping for me.

As soon as I arrived at the conference site, I began relaying my vision to the other speakers of the conference. When I began to speak of it, though, I suddenly had another vision. I saw all seven ladies standing with me, and all of us were wearing "No Fear" shirts. I quickly shared the vision with the seven women and we all said, "Well, let's go for it. Let's do it." Another faithful husband was dispatched to the mall armed with instructions to find seven "No Fear" shirts.

When I got back home after that first meeting that night, I found laid out on the kitchen counter, not only a "No Fear" T-shirt, but also a "No Fear" hat. I looked on the inside rim, and printed there was the phrase, "Don't let your fears stand in the way of your dreams." I knew at that point that God would grant us victory! I went to bed excited and anxious, watching to see what God was about to do.

The next morning before the meeting, Jim told me of a dream the Lord gave him that night to be released during my session: "I've had a vision that has materialized; I've seen eight women carving out a new beginning. If the women will shed their apparel called 'No Fair,' they will be given something from Heaven that some have said only men can wear: a name that says 'No Fear.' Trade in the old 'No Fair' deal, and cash in where there is nothing to fear. No fear!'" I felt that the Lord was giving me the stones I needed for my sling to slay the giant named intimidation. The time for confrontation was at hand.

Finally, the morning session began and I called the seven other women to the front of the auditorium. All eight of us stood before a large crowd of women wearing our "No Fear" T-shirts. I wore my shirt backwards, so the words printed on the back, "Fear Nothing!" were printed across my heart. I wore my hat with the words written inside, "Don't let your fears stand in the way of your dreams," guarding and encircling my mind. I read the word Jim had given me earlier that morning. I could sense God's warring angels all around the auditorium, and I could feel the anger of God toward the devil for the many ways he had hurt and abused these women. The atmosphere was electric! I declared, "God has set the day of deliverance!" The effect was spectacular! The ladies in that meetings were able to instantly take the word of the Lord as their own, and many, many women were set free and empowered with a bold and courageous spirit—the very Spirit of God!

As I worked on this chapter, I was reminded that I am the most unlikely candidate to be writing something like this! The only reason that I can write these words is because of the transforming power of the love and grace that God extended toward me. I had always been very conservative and reserved, and I felt like I was constantly battling intimidation. It just made me sick, and I hated it. There was much in me that wanted to come out, but I felt like there were chains wrapped around my ankles. I felt like a champion runner who couldn't run because I was all chained up and bound on the inside.

Setting the Captives Free

I cried out for years, "Lord, I just want to be so totally sold out and consumed with You that this fear thing gets completely annihilated so I won't even have it anymore." I thank God for hearing and answering my prayers. I've learned that God is jealous for a relationship with each one of us. He is angry at the enemy for draping cloaks of comparison and intimidation over us. They have nearly choked the life breath out of us. God is standing up and warring on our behalf today. He is setting the captives free and releasing them into the creativity He ordained for them from the beginning.

This even applies to those of us who are succumbing to pressure to dress like everybody else. It is time for us to set our own fashion standards. We weren't called to be like everybody else; we were called to be the unique person God fashioned us to be. Some of us have it so bad that we actually look at other people's plates in buffet lines just to make sure we don't take more than anyone else. We don't want to "stick out." Many of us can't even walk across a room without wondering, What is everybody thinking as I walk across the room? God's answer is direct and to the point:

> *For God did not give us a spirit of timidity (of cowardice, of craven and cringing and fawning fear), but [He has given us a spirit] of power and of love and of calm and well-balanced mind and discipline and self-control* (2 Timothy 1:7 AMP).

> *There is no fear in love [dread does not exist], but full-grown (complete, perfect) love turns fear out of doors and expels every trace of terror! For fear brings with it the thought of punishment, and [so] he who is afraid has not reached the full maturity of love [is not yet grown into love's complete perfection]* (1 John 4:18 AMP).

God has been wonderful to me. He has been working on my intimidation and fear problems for years. Jim would be traveling around the world while I was at home caring for four small children and handling home schooling, the ministry finances, and everything else around the house. When he would come home from these trips and say, "Ann, God really came down and it was so wonderful," I wanted to say, "I don't want to hear it, Jim. I've been changing diapers and home schooling kids. I have been the disciplinarian all week, and to tell you the truth, *I want God to show up here.*" Frankly, I was jealous.

I will never forget the day I leaned up against the wall and said, "Lord, I want so much to be with You, but I am so busy I just can't. I don't have time just to sit down and soak in Your Presence." The Lord gently told me, "Ann, I know that. I am the God of the impossible, and I tell you that what you think is impossible is *possible*. I am going to come to you in the night hours." That is when He began giving me dreams as never before. He was totally rearranging my perception of myself, of Him, and of how I thought He felt about me. To my surprise, I began to discover that the God of the universe actually longed for me.

I Choose You!

One of my most significant dreams was about "number 29," a number that has come to mean "being chosen" to me. I dreamed that I had entered a large royal court where the king's court was scheduled to open in session. There was a woman there who hated me with a passion. She put cigarette ashes on my head, and would do anything to shame me. I was assigned the number 29 when I entered the king's court, but as I waited for the court to open, I noticed that someone was calling out women's numbers. If your number was picked, then you had to go spend the night with a man—whether you wanted to or not. This woman who hated me so much called out my number! Rather than submit to the sickening prospect of spending the night with a strange man, I ran out of the court.

I didn't know it, but at the same time, the preliminary foolishness with the women's numbers had stopped because the king's son had come out into the royal court. He was going to pick his bride that day, and they were calling for a number to select the prince's bride. It was at that precise moment that the woman who hated me had called my number, number 29. The king's son looked up just as I ran out of the room. He put his finger up to his mouth and said, "I like that. She ran away from evil. I like it. *I choose her!*"

Everyone in the court began to ask one another, "Where did she go? Did you see where she went? The prince has chosen her." Then in my dream I saw myself come back out into the court, but this time I was dressed in regal clothes, and I looked totally different. I walked down the center aisle of the royal court, and the king's son kissed me and placed a royal scepter in my hand.

That dream wasn't just for me—it was for us, the Bride of Christ. He has chosen us. When the enemy comes against us to revile, intimidate, threaten, and entrap us, and we run from him, God says, "I choose them. I choose them!" We are chosen.

Shortly after the "number 29" vision, the Lord directed me to Esther 2:9, which tells how Hegai, the steward over King Ahasuerus' harem, gave Esther the most favored place in the harem.

And the maiden pleased [Hegai] and obtained his favor. And he speedily gave her the things for her purification and her portion of food and the seven chosen maids to be given her from the king's palace; and he removed her and her maids to the best [apartment] in the harem (Esther 2:9 AMP).

We have the most favored place too. God wants to remove the old information that says, "You are unworthy." He wants to remove the old programs that taught women, "You can never trust men because all they do is step on you." He wants to remove the intimidation and compulsive comparison that says, "I'll never lose that 20 pounds. I can't get up to their standards." God is saying, "Be yourself. I love you the way I made you. I created you the way you are, and I love you."

If you have sinned or failed in some way, confess it to Him. He is faithful and just to forgive you (see 1 Jn. 1:9). Do not be bound by mistakes of the past. If you've confessed it, God has forgotten it, so you are clean before Him.

God wants to woo and draw you into His Presence, and when He does, you will walk down that aisle to your Bridegroom with no shame on your face. You will be captivated by His love when He says, "Oh, how I've waited for you to come. How I've longed to embrace you and be in union with you." When you come into that place, all fear just melts away. No matter how much the enemy tries to come against you and intimidate you, he can't stand before the perfect love of God.

Intimidation will cause you to do things that you would not otherwise do. I had another dream that illustrates this point. My oldest son, Justin, was in this dream with me. We were in China, running food and clothing and other supplies to needy people. Somehow I knew we had to be careful not to spend one entire night in one place. We constantly moved from one place to another to foil the enemy's efforts to catch up with us.

Fleeing From the Hangman's Noose

We were getting ready to leave a house in the middle of the night, and Justin had left ahead of me in the company of one of our guides. I was still gathering up the remaining traces of clothing when enemy soldiers came in. They took me out to the yard where their ruler or king was waiting. He wanted to punish me by hanging me—but not to the point of death. He just wanted to hang me long enough to "punish" me, without killing me. At that point, I saw a couple in my dream who used to be a part of our church family. I understood them to symbolize faith in my life, because they had a strong gift of faith operating in their lives. The odd thing was that when this couple walked up to the yard, they both had visible rope burns on their necks.

I almost consented to the enemy ruler's punishment of letting me "almost" hang to death, but then I realized that the evil ruler could be tricking me! How foolish of me to trust my life to my enemy's hands. The problem was that I was intimidated. At first I thought, *Oh well, at least he doesn't want to really kill me. He just wants to hang me for a little while.* I realized that once the hangman's noose was around my neck and I was hanging above the ground, there would be no way for me to say, "Take it off! Take it off!" Who says you can trust the word of the enemy?

Instead of agreeing to the king's desired punishment, I began to preach the gospel to the king—totally free of intimidation! He was so intrigued that he let me continue. Then he led us into his court chamber room where approximately 50 chairs were grouped around a huge oval table. The string of chairs at the table went all the way across the front of the room on an elevated floor. Everything seemed to be dark and the furniture was very black. The other believers walked around the room praying quietly in tongues while I kept preaching the Word.

I felt that it was similar to Paul's situation when he preached to King Agrippa (see Acts 26:27-28). Then I pulled a rock from my shirt pocket that looked like some kind of uncut, unpolished gem or crystalline material. It was dark green in color, but as I spoke, the crystal grew and grew, and became a brilliant, glowing, almost iridescent stone.

In my dream, when the enemy king saw the light shining from the gem, he took the crystal in his hand and watched it continue to grow as I continued to preach the Word. He was holding a miracle, a wonder of God in his own hand, and he watched it grow with his own eyes.

When we are on the verge of a breakthrough, the enemy will always come by surprise and try to intimidate us, hoping to make us settle for something less than the total victory that we don't yet see. We need to press through and confront our enemy of intimidation. We need to allow the boldness of the Holy Spirit to come upon us like the light that began to shine through the gemstone in my dream. That light symbolizes the Word that is living and active, as it comes forth from within us.

Miracles—Visible to All

We are all "living stones" precious in God's sight (see 1 Pet. 2:5-6). As we stir up the gifts and callings within us and let the boldness of the Lord come out, we will begin to glow like uncut gems in the sunlight. We will become miracles visible to all. This is a good day to do business with God and with the enemy. This is a good day to decide that we're not going to let the enemy of intimidation strangle us anymore. It's time for every noose to come off, and it's time to bring the gems out of our pockets and see the miracle of God He wants to do in us.

Father, in the name of Jesus, we present ourselves to You. This day we choose to take the noose of intimidation off our necks. And in the name of Jesus we reject intimidation. We renounce the spirit of intimidation—whether it's in us or coming against us—we renounce it in the name of Jesus, and by the blood of the Lamb we break that power. We break the power of intimidation and the fear of man, in the name of Jesus Christ our Lord! In Jesus' name we pray, amen.

We need to begin to have confidence that we will hear what the Lord will speak to us in the days and nights ahead. We need to release the creative flow of the Holy Spirit over everyone in our families and local church bodies. We need to be who God has made us to be. We need to bloom, and blossom, and release our unique fragrances to the Lord. This will happen as we look neither to the left nor to the right, but keep our eyes fixed on Him. We need to let Him set the standard of what we speak, how we act, how we dress, and how we live our lives.

God has ordained that we live our lives under His banner of love, and beside it is our second banner of the Kingdom: *No More Fear!*

Bless the Lord—he whom the Lord sets free is free indeed! I agree with the psalmist who stated, "I sought the Lord, and He answered me, and delivered me from all my fears." Thank You, Lord, for deliverance from fear! Amen and amen.

Chapter 5

Receiving
the Father's Love

Jim W. Goll

But you, when you pray, go into your inner room, and when you have shut your door, pray to your Father who is in secret, and your Father who sees in secret will repay you. ...for your Father knows what you need, before you ask Him. Pray, then, in this way: "Our Father who art in heaven, hallowed be Thy name" (Matthew 6:6,8-9).

When the disciples asked Jesus to teach them how to pray, He told them to pray *to their Father* in Heaven. Since more than half of all American homes have been split and divided by divorce, this statement may well send chills through a large number of new believers who enter our church doors. For many of them, their earthly fathers were absent from their lives, or were forced by a court order to remain part-time fathers at best. The circumstances of our nation's family problems do not set aside the words of the Lord; it emphasizes them.

Everywhere we go, we meet Christians and non-Christians alike who long to know the heavenly Father's love. With more and more people coming to the cross of Christ bearing deep emotional and spiritual wounds, we are seeing a rise in the number of supernatural and miraculous encounters as our loving God moves to meet the needs of His children. Michal Ann and I felt that any book dealing with our supernatural God should also mention His role as our heavenly Father, who is full of mercy and compassion for those who have been hurt, wounded, and rejected. Some of the most glorious testimonies we have heard confirming His miraculous power occurred as God moved to reveal His Father's heart to brokenhearted or wounded members of His Body.

But there are obstacles in our pathway that need to be identified and removed in order for our pipeline to Heaven be clear and clean. The Lord wants us whole and free, able to receive and respond to His revelatory ways. How does this occur? First, we must understand God's compassionate nature.

Defining Compassion

The New Testament is filled with evidence of God's overwhelming love and compassion for us. According to the *Merriam-Webster Dictionary*, the word *compassion* refers to "a sympathetic consciousness of others' distress together with a desire to alleviate it."[1] *Vine's Expository Dictionary of Old and New Testament Words mentions four verbs and t*wo nouns that deal with compassion. The first verb, *oikteirō*, means "to have pity, a feeling of distress through the ills of others." It is used in reference to God's compassion (see Rom. 9:15). *Splanchnizomai* means "to be moved as to one's inwards, to be moved with compassion." It is frequently recorded of Christ toward the multitude and toward individual sufferers (see Mt. 9:36; Lk. 7:13). The third verb, *sumpatheō*, means "to suffer with another, to be affected similarly" (think of the English word *sympathy*), "to have 'compassion' upon" (see Heb. 10:34). *Eleeō* means "to have mercy, to show kindness, by beneficence" or assistance (see Mt. 18:33). As for the two nouns, *oiktirmos* and *splanchnon*, the first refers to the inward parts, the seat of emotion, while the latter means "compassions." The adjective *sumpathēs* denotes "suffering with" or "compassionate."[2]

The truth is that this English word doesn't begin to express the depth of God's love, yearning, and brokenness on our behalf. Ken Blue has said, "The kind of compassion Jesus was said to have for people was not merely an expression of His will but rather an eruption from deep within His being. Out of this compassion of Jesus sprang His mighty works of rescue, healing, and deliverance."[3] The only way to understand how much and how passionately our Father and His Son care about us is to look at His Word and the language He uses in it. Jesus had so much *compassion* for a widow who had lost her only son that He stopped the funeral procession and raised her son from the dead (see Lk. 7:12-15).

Jesus was so brokenhearted over the obstinate ways of Jerusalem that He wept over that city, knowing the ruin that would come upon it in the years after His death and resurrection. He said of her people, "How often I wanted to gather your children together, just as a hen gathers her brood under her wings, and you would not have it!" (Lk. 13:34b)

Jesus gave us a picture of His Father's love when He taught the disciples about prayer and the way our Father God answers them:

> *For everyone who asks, receives; and he who seeks, finds; and to him who knocks, it shall be opened. Now suppose one of you fathers is asked by his son for a fish; he will not give him a snake instead of a fish, will he? Or if he is asked for an egg, he will not give him a scorpion, will he? If you then, being evil, know how to give good gifts to your children, how much more shall your heavenly Father give the Holy Spirit to those who ask Him?* (Luke 11:10-13)

God Is Compassionate Toward Us

God wants to give you and I good gifts today, and the first and best gift of all is His fatherly love. The first step is to recognize His compassion toward us, and how He wants us to share it in turn with others. Psalm 145:9 says, "The Lord is good to all; He tell us, "But Thou, O Lord, art a God full of compassion, and gracious, longsuffering, and plenteous in mercy and truth" (Ps. 86:15 KJV).

When Jesus shared the story of the prodigal son in Luke 15, He was undoubtedly thinking of His own Father's compassion for His lost and wayward children on earth. You and I are the prodigals in this story, and God Himself is the loving Father running to meet us with great joy. In the parable of the good Samaritan in Luke 10, we see God's plan for you and I to share His love with others in practical and compassionate ways. It is clear that every believer is take for his own the calling of Jesus Christ in Isaiah 61:1-6, which Jesus quoted at the launch of His adult ministry in Luke 4:18-19.

> *The Spirit of the Lord God is upon me, because the Lord has anointed me to bring good news to the afflicted; He has sent me to bind up the brokenhearted, to proclaim liberty to captives, and freedom to prisoners;*
>
> *To proclaim the favorable year of the Lord, and the day of vengeance of our God; to comfort all who mourn,*
>
> *To grant those who mourn in Zion, giving them a garland instead of ashes, the oil of gladness instead of mourning, the mantle of praise instead of a spirit of fainting. So they will be called oaks of righteousness, the planting of the Lord, that He may be glorified.*
>
> *Then they will rebuild the ancient ruins, they will raise up the former devastations, and they will repair the ruined cities, the desolations of many generations.*
>
> *And strangers will stand and pasture your flocks, and foreigners will be your farmers and your vinedressers.*
>
> *But you will be called the priests of the Lord; you will be spoken of as ministers of our God. You will eat the wealth of nations, and in their riches you will boast.*
>
> (Isaiah 61:1-6)

The sixth verse tells us *who we are*. The first three verses tell us *what we do*, and the fourth and fifth verses tell us the supernatural results *of what we do*.

The Book of Hebrews tells us that the main reason Jesus is qualified to be our great High Priest is because He was "touched with the feeling of our infirmities" (Heb. 4:15 KJV). The Greek term used there, *sumpatheō*, stems from a root word that literally means "to experience pain jointly or of the same kind."[4] God has made us kings and priests as well, but the only way we can express and share our Father's love with others is for us to first experience it ourselves.

Good News for Wounded Hearts

The wonderful thing about God is that even as He trains and commissions us to carry His healing to others, He is healing us! We are asked in the Book of Proverbs, "The spirit of a man will sustain his infirmity; but a wounded spirit who can bear?" (Prov. 18:14 KJV) The New American Standard version puts it this way: "The *spirit* of a man can *endure* his *sickness*, but a *broken spirit* who can *bear*?"

Many people don't realize that we are "triune" or three-part beings, much like our Creator is. Man is an *eternal spirit* who has a *soul* and dwells in a physical *body*. Wounds and pain can come to any one of these areas. When we receive Christ as Lord and Savior, our spirit man is instantly and totally transformed into a new being in Christ. Our souls and bodies, however, must be re-trained and reformed more slowly over our lifetimes. This explains why it is possible for Christians to be sad, hurt, depressed, or angry. John Wimber, a noted Christian leader, shed some light on the way our different parts relate to one another:

> "While sickness of the spirit is caused by what we do, sickness of the emotions is generally caused by what is done to us. It grows out of the hurts done to us by other persons or some experience we have been exposed to in the past. These hurts affect us in the present, in the form of bad memories and weak or wounded emotions. This in

turn leads us into various forms of sin, depression, a sense of worthlessness and inferiority, unreasoning fears and anxieties, psychosomatic illnesses, etc. Included in these are the present-day effects of the sins of the parents in the bloodline of a person. Thus healing of past hurts touches the emotions, the memories, and the person's bloodline."[5]

The apostle Peter was clearly portrayed by the Gospels as a man who constantly wrestled with his impulsive nature, his lack of education or an impressive vocation, his violent temper, and at times, his weak character. He was quick to laugh or spring into action, but he would also bend to social and political pressure and was sometimes slow to forgive himself for his failures. It was Peter who boldly told Jesus he would never, ever deny Him (see Mt. 26:33). Yet it was Peter who publicly betrayed Jesus three times as Jesus listened nearby (see Mt. 26:74-75). Jesus confronted Peter after the resurrection and demonstrated His love for him when He told Peter to feed His sheep (see Jn. 21:16). It was Peter who wrote these words to us about living a godly life:

> *Grace and peace be multiplied to you in the knowledge of God and of Jesus our Lord; seeing that **His divine power has granted to us everything pertaining to life and godliness**, through the true knowledge of Him who called us by His own glory and excellence. For by these He has granted to us His precious and magnificent promises, in order that by them you might become partakers of the divine nature, having escaped the corruption that is in the world by lust* (2 Peter 1:2-4).

These words were written by divine inspiration, and they are true. God has given us everything we need to live lives that are pleasing to Him. Unfortunately, sometimes we don't realize that help is available to deal with the many problems we face in life.

There are three general conclusions agreed upon by nearly all experts:

1. People have problems that sometimes remain untouched by conversion, the baptism of the Holy Spirit, Bible study, and the personal prayer and devotional life of the individual.

2. Hidden in the recesses of the subconscious mind are hurts and wounds that are surrounded by feelings that still adversely affect the person's life in the present.

3. The focus of healing of past hurts is to release those hurtful memories in such a way that they no longer have a negative effect on the present or future of the individual. This is primarily done through the act of forgiveness.

These hidden hurts that seem to stick with us even after we are converted to Christ Jesus are inflicted on us through the effects of living in a fallen imperfect world, through the wounds inflicted on us by others, and through the sins of others who went before us. I'm glad to know that God is greater than them all, but godly wisdom and knowledge is needed here to achieve freedom in the Father.

Effects of Living in a Fallen World

All of us are subject to the effects of four major categories common to life in a fallen world. These categories include *incidents of history, accidents of nature, disease,* and *poverty*. One or more of these things affected every major character in the Bible, including God's only begotten Son. The wonderful thing is that these people overcame their afflictions and circumstances to obtain a good report in God. Jesus had to deal with incidents of history—His earthly father, Joseph, heeded an angel's warning and fled to Egypt to protect Jesus from a vengeful and jealous king. Jesus had to deal with the political ambitions of jealous Sadducees and Pharisees, and with the racial prejudices of His day.

Any one of us may be carrying hidden wounds suffered at the hands of others. These may stem from broken relationships or from the work of demonic forces in our family line because of the sin of parents or ancestors. Some of us suffer because of the criminal acts or behavior of others (such as sexual abuse, rape, physical abuse, etc.), or even prenatal rejections (which are so common today). Many of us become wounded because we enter the world thinking we have to perform or prove ourselves to society to earn love and respect, or because our parents forced unrealistic and demanding expectations on us. Nearly everyone admits to pain from their own wrong choices or failure to accept personal responsibility in certain areas. This in turn can lead to self-destructive bitterness, self-hate, and false expectations for ourselves and others. The truth is that we are a product of our decisions. What happens to us in life is not as important as how we respond to it.

God's Word and His eternal laws provide an anchor of stability and understanding in the midst of our confusing world. Some of His laws are eternal and will affect us all our lives whether they are broken or honored. These include *laws of retribution*, such as the commandment to honor our father and mother, which brings long life on the earth (see Deut. 5:16); to avoid judging others and thus avoid judgment ourselves (see Mt. 7:1-2); to remember that we reap what we sow (see Mt. 7:17; 13:1-23; Gal. 6:7). These also include the command to never hold others in bondage through unforgiveness (see Mt. 18:21-35).

God's *laws of healing* include His promises concerning giving and receiving mercy (see Lk. 6:36-38); the importance of confession and repentance of sin (see 1 Jn. 1:8-9); and the importance of ministering forgiveness to one another (see Jn. 20:23; Jas. 5:16).

Wounds, Failure, and God's Grace in the Bible

The Bible is filled with examples of how wrong decisions, sin, and failure affected peoples lives; and of how God's love and provision brought victory in spite of them. Michal, the daughter of King Saul and first wife of David, adopted a judgmental attitude toward David. It is true that her attitude was affected by her father's sin (his sin caused his demotion from the throne and led to the anointing of David as his successor). However, it was *her choice* to despise David for his unrestrained worship and praise of

God in public. As a result of her sin, Michal remained barren the rest of her life. (See Second Samuel 6.)

David's sin with Bathsheba led to serious consequences that brought immediate sorrow and lasting pain. First David and Bathsheba suffered the death of their illegitimate child, and the shadow of sexual excess and violence would strike his household repeatedly throughout his life (see 2 Sam. 12:18). David's son, Amnon, fell in love with his own step-sister, Tamar, and then raped her. Another son, Absalom, murdered his step-brother, Amnon, in revenge for his sin against Tamar. Absalom ultimately rebelled against his own father, King David, and publicly committed adultery with David's wives in fulfillment of prophecy (see 2 Sam. 16:22). Then David's son, Solomon, who ascended the throne after him, fell in total failure as a result of unrestrained sexual desire and love for ungodly women, despite God's unequaled deposit of wisdom in him (see 1 Kings 11:1-8).

The Book of Genesis describes the many adversities *Joseph* faced in his life. The youngest son of Israel (formerly called Jacob), Joseph made his brothers jealous through his unwise communication of God's spiritual revelations, which led to his being sold into slavery. He dealt with this tragic betrayal by forgiving his brothers, thus escaping the dangers of bitterness. He wept when he finally met his brothers again, which brought further healing through healthy emotional release. Joseph was also able to reinterpret his hurtful experience *in the light of the purposes of God*, and thus was freed of any negative effects from his bad memories (see Gen. 45:7-8). It is interesting to see that Joseph's bad experiences with Potiphar's wife and the imprisonment it produced did not seem to affect him much! He seemed to forgive easily because he saw these happenings in the light of God's plan. Indeed, the Bible repeatedly says "...the Lord was with him..." (see Gen. 39:2,20-23).

The *two disciples* who encountered the resurrected Christ on the road to Emmaus in Luke 24 were the picture of individuals trying to deal with the pain of numbing disappointment and disillusionment. Jesus entered their emotional world by talking with them, listening to their story, and then exposing their memories of failure and frustration to a new and positive light. He showed them how their despondency was caused by their failure to understand the purposes of God and by their lack of faith in the Scriptures (see Lk. 24:25-26). Then He used those same Scripture passages to reinterpret their negative experience and bring new power and hope through revelation (see Lk. 24:27). The most powerful change of all came when the men had a personal revelation of their risen Lord.

I've already mentioned *Peter*, the only man to publicly deny Jesus three times, and the only man to walk on water with the Lord. His life is a continual picture of human failure redeemed and restored through divine love, forgiveness, and faithfulness. Jesus clearly warned Peter that satan wanted to exploit his weaknesses, but He reassured him that He was faithfully praying and interceding for him (see Lk. 22:31-32). We can be confident and take hope today because Jesus is doing the very same thing for us as He prays and intercedes at the Father's right hand day and night (see Heb. 2:17-18; 7:25-26).

The Effects of Forgiveness and Unforgiveness

Jesus made it clear in His parable of the unforgiving servant that we must learn how to forgive others unconditionally, no matter what the circumstance (see Mt. 18:15-35; 5:23-24). We must be quick to forgive, no matter who is in the wrong or how bad it hurts. We must learn to forgive and forget, just as God has forgiven us (see Eph. 4:32). Consider these two statements and model your life accordingly:

1. *Forgiveness is God's chief and greatest remedy for what ails us!* The reason we *must* forgive is because unforgiveness always comes back on *us*. Unforgiveness and bitterness can be traced to almost every disease and life-shortening plague in the human experience. Although not all diseases are caused by unforgiveness, unforgiveness can and does manifest itself through them all. And forgiveness can almost

always boost the body's ability to fight disease, fatigue, and effects of life's struggles.

2. *Unforgiveness* is satan's chief and greatest tool to bring torment and misery to the human race! Remember, we determine our progress by how we respond to the circumstances of this life. Unforgiveness gives keys to the devil that unlock his dark slaves to wreak havoc in our lives. Don't give the devil the key to your life!

God's Three-Part Remedy

The Lord's remedy for our wounds includes a gift, a service, and a command. First, He gave us His Son, Jesus Christ, who came to "heal the brokenhearted" and "set at liberty them that are bruised" (Lk. 4:18 KJV). You must acknowledge that Jesus took *your* pain and carried *your* sorrows on the cross of Calvary. He has accomplished it all! This is God's *gift* to us; it's something we can't earn. Receive the gift.

Second, He provided us with the Holy Spirit, whom Jesus called the "finger of God" (Lk. 11:20). One of the services or roles of the Holy Spirit is to reveal the mind of God to us, and to point out any bitterness, hurts, wounds, or rejection hidden within us. God, the Holy Spirit, knows all things; and it is through His work within us that we are conformed to the image of Jesus Christ. It is the Holy Spirit who will guide us to all truth (see Jn. 16:13). We must allow the Great Physician in the form of the Holy Spirit to diagnose our problem before a cure can be pronounced. Let Him service His Body and point out the specifics in detail.

Third, one of the most important ingredients for healing and health in our spirits, souls, and bodies is a *command*. It is *forgiveness*. I tell people around the world that God's great remedy for wounded spirits consists of three words: *Forgive, forgive, forgive!* It may be ironic, but it is definitely true: The first person to suffer, and the one who suffers the most from unforgiveness, is *you*. And the first person to be blessed, and the one who receives the most benefit from forgiveness, is *you*! God issues a *command*. Forgive.

Forgiveness involves recognizing that *you* have been totally forgiven by God (even though you didn't deserve it). It also involves releasing any person from the "debt" you feel he or she owes you for offending or hurting you (even though you feel he or she doesn't deserve it). Finally, you must accept the person who offended you just as that person is. Release the other individual from the responsibility of having to meet your needs in any way. Forgive, forget, and get on with your life in Christ. (That also means you must forgive *yourself*!)

Of course, there are specialized situations in some cases that require more specific ministry. These situations involve people who feel that they are being affected by the power of inherited spiritual family conditions such as chronic alcoholism, sexual perversion, child molestation, and other types of social and emotional abuse. (Unfortunately, this pattern is reaching epidemic proportions in our society.) These spiritual influences must be renounced and broken in the name of Jesus, and the truth of God's Word ministered under the guidance of the Holy Spirit. In other situations, there are some ungodly "soul ties" or emotional dependencies that have a negative effect on believers' lives. These dependencies must also be renounced and broken in the name of Jesus. In all these cases, additional Bible teaching and compassionate counseling, the ministry of deliverance, and support from a caring group of people will help the believers begin new lives free of oppression through the power of the Holy Spirit.

Dealing With Rejection

By far, the most prevalent cause of broken hearts and spiritual wounds is *rejection*. I define *rejection* as "a sense of being unwanted or the sense that although you want people to love you, no one does," and "the feeling of wanting to be a part of a group but feeling excluded—somehow always being on the outside looking in." I read one time that one out of five people in the U.S. have been affected by rejection. Depending on how they defined "affected," I think they could raise that figure to one out of one!

People suffering from rejection often come from a single-parent family where one parent left or was separated from them through divorce. Many marriages are dysfunctional in nature, which results in scars on the offspring. These children will often admit to suffering from chronic loneliness or depression, and some advance to stages of rebellion with its various bad fruit. Many of them have made proclamations about themselves at one time or another, "I wish I was dead," or "I hate myself." An alarming number of these people have either thought seriously of committing suicide, or actually attempted to do so. Patience, kindness, and great love are needed here. The opposite of rejection is acceptance, and that is exactly what God offers each and every one of us through His Son, Jesus Christ.

Regardless of whether rejection begins through illegitimate birth, poverty, parental rejection, family problems, unfair comparisons with others, or through self-rejection due to physical characteristics, the results tend to follow predictable patterns. Unfortunately, for every negative emotion, reaction, and attitude, there can be a corresponding demonic spirit. Most people tend to react to the pain of rejection internally where no one can see it. Others respond externally in ways that anyone can see it. Whichever the case may be, the remedies are basically the same. We must submit all patterns of darkness to God's light.

Internal reactions to rejection include increased loneliness, self-pity, depression or moodiness, outright despair, despondency, and a sense of hopelessness. These strongholds of the mind eventually result in death wishes and persistent thoughts of suicide. These are particularly dangerous because they are often hidden from the eyes of friends or family members who might be willing and able to help.

Typical external reactions to rejection can easily be spotted in many teenagers who are struggling to find their way through adolescence, but if the causes are not dealt with, these so-called "adolescent" reactions may well turn into lifelong life patterns that lead to failure, more rejection, pain for others, and ultimately death. Some people resort to *hardness* to conceal their pain. They may react to rejection by snarling, "So what?! Who needs them anyhow?" Others become *indifferent*. They would say, "I don't care! Nobody is ever going to hurt me again. I'll put up a barrier so no one will ever get through, that's what I'll do." The most important thing they will ever do is admit that *they* are in need—we all are! We must become vulnerable again to be healed. Facing pain is one of the first steps to wholeness. Then, in this state of transparency, they are enabled to receive the love of God, a new name, and an identity in Christ. They really can "start over."

A few move beyond hardness and indifference, though, to *rebellion*. They feel things will be better if they aggressively seek power over the forces or people they think are "against" them. (This usually means some authority such as their parents, God, the Church, Christians, or any court, judge, law enforcement officer or anyone else who dares to challenge their actions.) An even more deadly stage of this rebellion is involvement in *witchcraft*, the ultimate religion of rebellion and illicit power. In today's perverse society, this often results in prolonged drug use and other self-abusive reactions and addictions. The final external reaction against rejection is permanent and tragic, and that is suicide—*death*.

The Remedy

In every one of these cases, "the way of the Cross leads home." No one was rejected more than Jesus, and yet He forgave all mankind for the rejection and mistreatment He received. Jesus was even rejected by His own Father in Heaven as a necessary part of the divine plan for the redemption of man (see Mt. 27:46; Hab. 1:3). Jesus didn't die from His wounds or from the brutality of His crucifixion—He died of a broken heart. His heart was broken for us so that we could be healed!

Let's review a few pointers in procuring our healing or helping another achieve his healing.

1. *Turn on the search light of the Spirit of God.* Let the Lord specifically point out the bitterness, hurts, wounds, and

rejections that may be hidden in your life. Don't try to conjure it up; let Him bring it to your remembrance.

2. *Forgive!* Specifically forgive the person or persons who caused that hurt. Remember, forgiveness is an act of your will. It releases people from the debt they owe you for the offense, and accepts them as they are, releasing those people from the responsibility of meeting your needs.

3. *Repent from your own anger or bitterness.* Take personal responsibility for your reactions and repent. Then forgive yourself and release God to work in your life.

A Clean Pipeline

Our salvation and deliverance from rejection is found in the love of Jesus. God doesn't merely "tolerate" us; He fully *accepts us.* He always has time for us. Once we lay down all our bitterness and unforgiveness for others, once we give all our hurts to Him and receive the joy and acceptance He offers us through Jesus, we will be free to walk in supernatural power to set others free. It is at that point that we can begin to receive and respond to supernatural encounters with our supernatural God with wholeness. Let the healing come. And may close encounters with the Father's love begin.

> *Right now I ask for a revelation of the great grace of God in my life. I believe that the Father is for me and that Jesus Christ died for my sins. By His shed blood, I am forgiven and cleansed from all unrighteousnss. Heaven is my home. God is my Father. Jesus Christ is my older brother. I am a member of the best family on earth. I am not rejected but accepted. I am a vessel of destiny. I receive the love that the Father has for me. Bless You, Lord! Amen.*

Endnotes

1. *Merriam-Webster's Collegiate Dictionary*, 10th ed. (Springfield, Massachusetts: Merriam-Webster, Inc., 1994), **compassion** (n), 234.

2. W.E. Vine, *Vine's Complete Expository Dictionary of Old and New Testament Words* (Nashville: Thomas Nelson Publishers, 1985).

3. Ken Blue, *The Authority to Heal* (Downers Grove Illinois: InterVarsity Press, 1987), 76-77.

4. James Strong, *Strong's Exhaustive Concordance of the Bible* (Peabody, Massachusetts: Hendrickson Publishers, n.d.) **to be touched with** (Greek, #4834, #4835, #4841).

5. John Wimber, *Signs and Wonders Syllabus MC 511* (Anaheim, California: Vineyard Ministries International, 1985).

Chapter 6

This Means War!

Michal Ann Goll

*Fight the good fight of the faith; lay hold of the eternal life
to which you were summoned and [for which] you confessed the good confession [of faith] before many witnesses* (1 Timothy 6:12 AMP).

"Well gee, Ann. When are you and Jim going to start having
kids?" This seems like a very harmless remark, but in the midst
of our long struggle with infertility, it hurt. Yet it was this very
struggle that first catapulted me headlong into violent warfare.

War isn't something you ask for; it's something you are faced
with—usually against your will. You don't expect it; it just seems
to fall into your lap (or on your head). Jim often says, "We were
born in war and born for war." Well, I wasn't looking for trouble,
trials, and extra hurdles to jump over in this life. In my younger
days, I was very compliant. I hated confrontation of any kind (and
I still do), and I was the last person you would choose to write a
chapter on war.

When Jim and I got married, we automatically assumed that
we would have children. I always wanted to have children and I
took it for granted that it would happen. We assumed, along with
most Americans, that we would do our part to prove the statistics

accurate and produce 2.4 children (whatever that is), and own a home with two cars in the driveway. We assumed this until we discovered that we could not have children. At that point, we endured an endless cycle of medical tests, questions, outpatient visits, and trips to our infertility specialist. I underwent two surgeries in hopes of "fixing" whatever was wrong. The common threads through all this were that they were always extremely embarrassing, and they were all hopeless. Eventually we found out through our infertility specialist that my condition was very unusual and that there was no medical solution.

We exhausted every avenue that we could think of in our search for an answer to our very private problem. Above all we prayed. We asked God and we asked God; then we would rebuke our barrenness and speak God's Word over our bodies. We did everything we knew to do physically, medically, and spiritually. After six years, though, all attempts ended up in the same place—with no children.

It was incredibly painful. Jim and I were part of a small church in a college campus town. We spent those difficult years talking and counseling with a lot of college students—students who just kept falling in love, asking Jim to perform their wedding ceremonies, and then asking us to pray over their kids as they easily came. Meanwhile, our house was empty except for the two very disappointed people who lived in it.

We spent six long years in this valley of suffering, and Jim and I just didn't know what more to do. We reached a point where we were so discouraged that we had no more comfort to lend to each other, let alone much of anything to offer to anyone else. One day we retreated to "our own little corners" in our pain. Jim went for a solitary walk and I stayed in the house. We were apart, but our destination was the same. In our pain, we were both running to the Lord to ask Him again about all this.

Two years before Jim and I realized just how serious out situation was, Jim had received a dream from the Lord in which He said, "You will have a son and his name will be called Justin."

But every day brought me new agony as I saw woman after woman experience the joys of pregnancy and the arrival of a child. If this period of pain taught us anything, it taught us the value of what Jim calls "holy tenacious prayer." We had the Word of God, we had a fresh, direct word from the Lord through Jim's dream, and we had multitudes of friends who were praying with us. Nevertheless, the situation in the natural looked entirely hopeless.

You Must Fight for Your Children

I was more desperate than I had ever been in my life. "Lord, I really want to have children, and You know that I do. But if it's Your will for us not to have children, then I will surrender my will to You...I won't like it, but I will surrender myself to Your will for my life." It was almost as though He was waiting for me to say that, because He immediately responded, "Ann, I appreciate your attitude, but I'm not requiring that of you. *You are going to have to fight for your children.*"

As soon as I heard the Lord say those words, I was filled with the revelation that the Lord was feeling my pain, and that He longed for me to have children more than I did! He was pulling for me! I became aware that I had been blaming God for being childless, and the blame really belonged to satan. So I took a stand and made a proclamation that day. I said, "From this day forward, I'll no longer blame God for my infertility. I take the blame off God my Father, and put it squarely where it belongs— on the devil!" When I had finished, it seemed as though an ax was laid to the root of a large tree, and that significant damage had been done! I was filled with new hope, and with a fighting spirit.

Jim began to study every reference to barren women in the Bible, and he discovered that every barren woman in the Bible who was miraculously healed gave birth to either a prophet of God, or a deliverer of a nation! Hope began to spring up again as we prepared to enter our seventh year of our marriage. It was medically impossible for us to conceive, but God heard our cries of desperation. Even in our barrenness, God was about to bring forth that which was impossible.

In the midst of our trial, Mahesh Chavda conducted a healing service at the church that we were pastoring in Warrensburg, Missouri, and he issued a call for barren women to come forward. With the encouragement of friends, Jim and I eagerly jumped at the chance to receive prayer. When Mahesh placed his hands on us and prayed, the healing grace of God flooded my body as we were both overwhelmed by the Spirit's Presence. (In fact, I know God performed a restorative miracle of some kind—He created or recreated something that was inoperative before!) It was in our seventh year of marriage that our firstborn son, Justin, came into the world on the Day of Atonement that fall. (This occurred in spite of the opinions of some the best medical minds we could find.) The Lord has been faithful. Today we have four healthy, good-looking kids, but we had to wage intense spiritual battles for every single one of them.

The Fight Goes On!

I am still fighting for my children, but not only for my physical children. As I learned how to conduct warfare in the very practical issue of having children, I also saw other areas of spiritual conflict and entered the battle on behalf of others. I feel that in a very real sense I am battling on your behalf today. God has placed a "warring spirit" within me to deliver vital knowledge, help, and encouragement to you to continue on and become more like Christ.

For several years prior to the writing of this book, I've known that this experience wasn't just for my physical children. I began to realize that God had imparted His heart to me in the form of a tiny mustard seed to fight for His children. He was training me to wage war in the Spirit for those who are bound up by fear, shame, or condemnation, and to proclaim liberty to the captives and the favorable year of the Lord.

I'm still learning how to fight. I have not "arrived" by any means, but I am convinced that you and I are in a war. You cannot pick the time that you will go into battle. You don't always have that choice. In times of war, if you become sick or feel weak, you cannot say, "Okay, I'm going to go and lie down and check out because I really need some time out now." You do not have that option because the enemy does not play fair (and we shouldn't either!). We need to take advantage of the enemy, wherever and whenever we can.

An army doesn't go out to war in a haphazard manner. Its troops are very organized. They know their goals and the key details of their mission; they are aware of the limitations of their authority. Their great key is that they know their commander, and they cooperate with the chain of command. They know where the battleground is, their objective, their enemy, his weaponry, and his troop strength. The wise army also is keenly aware of his own weaknesses. In modern warfare, commanders know how much air cover they have and which units are operating in territory under hostile skies.

Spiritual warfare is no different. How do we prepare ourselves for battle in the heavenlies? You make yourself clean before the Lord. Why? Because the enemy is "the accuser of our brethren" who, according to Revelations 12:10 (AMP), "...keeps bringing before our God charges against them day and night...."

Where is the battleground? There is definitely a battlefield of the mind, because Paul spoke of "taking every thought captive to the obedience of Christ" (2 Cor. 10:5b). The battle is won or lost at the threshold of the mind. We must learn to dismiss the power of negativism and the enemy's device of the power of suggestion.

The Work of the Cross

What weapons does the enemy use? Satan makes heavy use of guilt, lies, and innuendo to accuse and entangle the saints. Among his many other kinds of weaponry are fear, shame, sickness, and temptation.

What weapons do I have? The apostle Paul described our heavy artillery in his Epistle to the Colossians:

And you who were dead in trespasses and in the uncircumcision of your flesh (your sensuality, your sinful carnal nature), [God] brought to life together with [Christ], having

*[freely] forgiven us all our transgressions, having can-
celed and blotted out and wiped away the handwriting of
the note (bond) with its legal decrees and demands which
was in force and stood against us (hostile to us). This
[note with its regulations, decrees, and demands] He set
aside and cleared completely out of our way by nailing it
to [His] cross. [God] disarmed the principalities and
powers that were ranged against us and made a bold display and public example of them, in triumphing over them
in Him and in it [the cross]* (Colossians 2:13-15 AMP).

Our transgressions are forgiven and our guilt and debt have
been blotted out. That means that when satan comes against us
trying to bring guilt on us, we don't have to take it because we
have been forgiven. Jesus Christ has disarmed the principalities
and powers. It is finished—perfectly complete. Jesus has already
done it! He made a bold display and a public example of them in
triumphing over them through the cross.

So we can triumph. In fact, we have an invitation to reign with
Him and can join the ranks of Heaven in celebrating His victory
over the enemy. We rejoice in the finished work of the cross. Paul
wrote, "But thanks be to God, Who in Christ always leads us in
triumph [as trophies of Christ's victory] and through us spreads
and makes evident the fragrance of the knowledge of God everywhere" (2 Cor. 2:14 AMP). We can be a testimony and witness to
Christ without even having to say a word because the fragrance of
Jesus is released through us. It will be noticed by people everywhere we go! The Scripture passage above says that we are His
trophies! Isn't it amazing?

Postures of Warfare

Through the cross of Calvary, and Christ's resurrection from
the dead, the battle has been won. But in some mysterious manner, Jesus has commissioned His followers to enforce the victory
of Calvary. Paul, the apostle, told the Ephesians:

*For we are not wrestling with flesh and blood [contending
only with physical opponents], but against the despotisms,*

against the powers, against [the master spirits who are] the world rulers of this present darkness, against the spirit forces of wickedness in the heavenly (supernatural) sphere. Therefore put on God's complete armor, that you may be able to resist and stand your ground on the evil day [of danger], and having done all [the crisis demands], to stand [firmly in your place] (Ephesians 6:12-13 AMP).

The "postures" of warfare include the defensive posture and the offensive posture, but they can be easily confused. We need to understand that though the enemy may come against us so strongly at times that we feel overpowered, God sees our stubborn stand as an *offensive* posture. God is pleased when we hold our ground no matter what circumstance we find ourselves in. We refuse to give up any ground. We now proclaim the blood of Jesus and the strength of God's Word, and that can be an incredibly aggressive act. There have been times in my life when I was in a place of physical weakness and it seemed that the enemy was attacking me with all his might. All I could do was say, "Lord, I feel so weak that I can't do anything, *but I know this...*."

For though we walk (live) in the flesh, we are not carrying on our warfare according to the flesh and using mere human weapons. For the weapons of our warfare are not physical [weapons of flesh and blood], but they are mighty before God for the overthrow and destruction of strongholds (2 Corinthians 10:3-4 AMP).

I remember hearing the international Bible teacher Derek Prince say that one of the most vulnerable places we have is our backside. That is why we are our brother's keeper—we are to watch out for one another. It is interesting that Psalm 18:40 says of the Lord, "Thou hast also made my enemies turn their backs to me...." No matter how powerful or formidable your enemy may appear to be, as you persevere, your God will cause them to turn their backs to you. He will reveal their mortal weakness to you and put victory in your hand.

I Call You to Be Witnesses

The Lord once spoke to my heart saying, "If you will separate yourself unto Me, if you will spend time before Me in quietness, I will feed you. I will give you the confidence that you need, and I will bring strength to you as you spend time alone with Me." I knew in my heart that this was to be linked directly to the Lord's words in Acts 1:8b: "And you shall be My *witnesses* both in Jerusalem, and in all Judea and Samaria, and even to the remotest part of the earth." There is a principle at work here. Your closest moments of intimacy are your highest moments of effective warfare. Time alone soaking in His Presence will make effective witnesses out of us.

What does the word *witnesses* refer to? The original Greek word for "witness" is *martus*, or "martyr." This word was applied to anyone who presented an unwavering testimony and life in demonstration of the gospel of Jesus Christ. Later on, the original term, *martyr*, was reserved for witnesses who gave their lives for the sake of Christ, while *witness* was used to describe those who took a firm stand but were not required to lose their lives in the process.

A witness is a living, full-time, full-color demonstration that the gospel is true and that Jesus Christ is risen. There is no better example of the truth of the gospel than your life lived in transparent honesty, leaning wholly on His strength and provision. Our lives carry much more of an impact than what we realize. As we make our way through this world, working, buying, selling, raising our children, and going in and out among our neighbors and co-workers, we carry with us the sweet aroma of Jesus. We have to believe Him. That fragrance of Christ permeates our being, and it goes everywhere we go. This is all part of the Lord's strategy to take His glory around the world.

Peter specifically said, "...if any of [your own husbands] are disobedient to the word, they may be won *without a word* by the behavior of their wives" (1 Pet. 3:1b). When Jesus said, "...be My *witnesses* both in Jerusalem, and in all Judea and Samaria, and even to the remotest part of the earth" (Acts 1:8b), He was telling us, "Be witnesses for Me *wherever you are*. Start where you are and go from there." It doesn't matter whether you are cleaning your kids' rooms, changing the oil in a car, doing computer work, or litigating a court case; remind yourself, "I am God's witness right here, right now. His aroma is here because I am here. I take Him wherever I go." As you do that, you are extending your circle of influence farther and farther beyond your home base.

Victory in the Blood and the Testimony

And they have overcome (conquered) him by means of the blood of the Lamb and by the utterance of their testimony... (Revelation 12:11 AMP).

Our two greatest weapons of warfare are the blood of Jesus and our ability to give our personal testimony about God's faithfulness in our lives. No one can counter or void what we have personally experienced in Christ. We can't be talked out of it, bullied out of it, or threatened out of our grasp on eternal life in Christ. The blood was shed by Christ and cannot be annulled by man or devil. This is why these are our two great overcoming power weapons. These are the ultimate "big guns" in the war of the heavens.

Considering the power contained in our word of testimony, it should be no surprise to us that the enemy of our souls has relentlessly assaulted the Body of Christ through his endless accusations to bring guilt and condemnation to us. Consider his motives. He wants to silence our testimony at all costs. The easiest way to do this is to make us feel like we have no testimony because of guilt and condemnation.

Although I don't want to glorify or magnify satan in any way, we must also realize that the apostle Paul said, "...we are not ignorant of his schemes" (2 Cor. 2:11). I don't want anyone reading this book to be ignorant or unaware of satan's favorite ploy of belittlement and harassment. Listen, we don't have a testimony because we are perfect; we have a testimony because *Jesus is perfect*, and we are wrapped up in Him!

I have talked to countless numbers of Christians over the years who have been assaulted with condemning thoughts in their minds. As a result, they felt degraded and unworthy of God's love. The enemy seemed to be taunting them and suggesting, "Who do you think you are? Why don't you just go hide in a cave—that's where you belong anyway. You are just a failure." My friend, if this is your situation, I want to tell you that it is time to declare war! Begin by reminding yourself of Paul's unforgettable words:

> *Concerning this* [thorn] *I entreated the Lord three times that it might depart from me. And He has said to me, "My grace is sufficient for you, for power is perfected in weakness." Most gladly, therefore, I will rather boast about my weaknesses, that the power of Christ may dwell in me. Therefore I am well content with weaknesses, with insults, with distresses, with persecutions, with difficulties, for Christ's sake; for when I am weak, then I am strong* (2 Corinthians 12:8-10).

That should send the accuser packing. The enemy will try to hamper you by weakening your confidence in the Lord or by negating your testimony. Remember this: The strength of your testimony is rooted in God's eternal faithfulness, not in your own ability or righteousness. You *do* have a testimony, and it is founded and rooted in Christ Jesus, who is glorified even in our weaknesses and shortcomings.

Armies Go to War Together

> *Two are better than one, because they have a good [more satisfying] reward for their labor; for if they fall, the one will lift up his fellow. But woe to him who is alone when he falls and has not another to lift him up! ... And though a man might prevail against him who is alone, two will withstand him. A threefold cord is not quickly broken* (Ecclesiastes 4:9-10,12 AMP).

It's time for this army to march to war arm in arm. This is not the time to be alone. We need each other. I feel that this is very strategic for our times. The Scriptures talk a great deal about our spiritual armor, but did you notice that it doesn't mention anything about our backside? I know some preachers claim that's because God's army doesn't run, but it's not the "running" I'm talking about; it's the backstabbing, underhanded enemy who does most of his warfare in darkness that I'm thinking about. The answer is found in the Scripture passage I just quoted from the Book of Ecclesiastes. "But woe to him who is alone when he falls and has not another to lift him up" (Eccles. 4:10b AMP).

We must come together and do battle in unity of mind and spirit under the banner of God's great love and the power of the name of Jesus. We need to watch out for one another—not in *fear* but in *wisdom*. I really feel like we are living in a season when the enemy has specifically targeted the Body of Christ with accusations and belittling condemnation. God wants us to come into a new realization of the power in the blood of Jesus and the power of the word of our testimony.

The Blood That Speaks

But you have come to Mount Zion and to the city of the living God, the heavenly Jerusalem, and to myriads of angels, to the general assembly and church of the firstborn who are enrolled in heaven, and to God, the Judge of all, and to the spirits of righteous men made perfect, and to Jesus, the mediator of a new covenant, and to the sprinkled blood, which speaks better than the blood of Abel (Hebrews 12:22-24).

The writer of Hebrews paints an exciting picture of our eternal destination, of the angels, of our companions in the Church of the firstborn, of our Father, and of Jesus our Savior and Mediator. Then he tells us how we will get there in the first place. It is only through "*the sprinkled blood, which speaks* better than the blood of Abel.*"

If you really want to understand the power of the blood, you have to go all the way back to the beginning. That is where every spiritual battle begins. Genesis chapter 4 tells us how Cain became jealous of his brother Abel when his sacrifice to God was accepted while Cain's was rejected. These were the first two sons of the first couple created by God—they were literally the generation of the future. Cain became so overcome by his jealousy and anger that he viciously killed Abel in the field and tried to cover up his crime. (Some things never change.) Look closely at the words of God:

> Then the Lord said to Cain, "Where is Abel your brother?" And he said, "I do not know. Am I my brother's keeper?" And He said, "What have you done? *The voice of your brother's blood is crying to Me from the ground*" (Genesis 4:9-10).

According to the Bible, *life is in the blood* (see Lev. 17:11). God's words to Cain tell us that when innocent blood is spilled in violence, it is able to cry out directly to God. The same God who is fully aware of every sparrow that will drop to the ground today and who knows the very number of hairs on our heads, is keenly tuned in to the voice of the blood (see Mt. 10:29-31). Two voices in particular picture the nature of our battle in the heavenlies. The reality is that Christ has *already* won every battle on earth and in Heaven, but we are expected to walk out that victory day by day, much like a "cleanup army" cleans out pockets of lingering resistance after a successful invasion. Our key weapon is found in the blood.

The blood of Abel seemed to cry out to God, "Vengeance! I want vengeance!" It became an eternal symbol of our race's fall into sin and the sentence of death. But before the presence of our Judge in Heaven, *there is a blood that speaks better than the blood of Abel.* What does this blood declare? The innocent blood of Jesus is a continuous reminder before our Father of the sacrifice of His precious Son. The blood of Jesus ever cries out, "Mercy! Mercy! Mercy be!"

Why Is It "the Sprinkled" Blood?

The second place we must go after the Garden of Eden is to the Holy of Holies of Moses' tabernacle and Solomon's temple.

Before the coming of Jesus the Messiah, the only way to receive atonement from sin was through the Law of Moses, the rules and guidelines laid down by God through Moses. Under this law, once a year the high priest of Israel would purify himself, minister to the Lord at the altar of incense (symbolic of the prayers of the saints), and then go beyond the veil of separation into the Most Holy Place.

Here the priest would take some of the blood of a sacrificed bull or goat and sprinkle it with his finger on the mercy seat (of the ark of the covenant), and on the horns of the altar—seven times each (see Lev. 16:14-18). The Law also says, "And with his finger he shall *sprinkle some of the blood* on it seven times, and cleanse it, and *from the impurities of the sons of Israel consecrate it*" (Lev. 16:19). The sad part about all this was that it had to be done every single year, and even then, the sins of Israel weren't *forgiven.* They were simply covered over or held in reserve until the Messiah would wash away all sin. Jesus the Messiah did come, and He willingly offered Himself as an innocent sacrifice and shed His blood for us. When He ascended on High, He became our High Priest and personally *sprinkled His blood* over our sins and permanently, totally, and eternally washed away and blotted out all our sins. Now do you see why Jesus' blood "speaks better" than Abel's?

Benefits of the Blood

I've already quoted this verse about the blood of the Lamb, but it is so important that I will quote it in full once again: "And they overcame him [the accuser of the brethren] because of the blood of the Lamb and because of the word of their testimony, and they did not love their life even to death" (Rev. 12:11 AMP). We overcome by testifying what the blood of Jesus has accomplished, and what it is accomplishing in our lives today. As you press through the enemy's mindless accusations and condemnations to fulfill your destiny in Christ, remind yourself and declare out loud the eternal benefits of the precious blood of the Lamb, Jesus Christ:

1. I have been forgiven through the *blood of Jesus* (see Heb. 9:22).

2. The *blood of Jesus* has cleansed me from *all* sin (see 1 Jn. 1:7).

3. I have been redeemed by the *blood of the Lamb* (see Eph. 1:7).

4. By *His blood*, I am justified ["just as if"] I have never sinned (see Rom. 5:9).

5. I have been sanctified [set apart] through *Jesus' blood* for a holy calling (see Heb. 13:12).

6. Peace has been made for me *through the blood of the cross* (see Col. 1:20).

7. I now have confidence to enter the Most Holy Place by the *blood of Jesus* (see Heb. 10:19).

Even though Jim and I have what many would call a "prayer ministry," I have to tell you that you will not prevail or win a spiritual battle through "prayer techniques," or even through past experience. There is no prayer "know-how" that will prevail over your demonic accuser—you prevail only through the blood of Jesus.

Charles Spurgeon once said, "Many keys fit many locks, but the master key is the blood and the name of Him that died and rose again, and ever lives in heaven to save unto the uttermost. The blood of Christ is that which unlocks the treasury of heaven."

My husband Jim wrote this prophetic exhortation in our training manual entitled, "Fire on the Altar," summarizing the benefits of the blood: "Plead the blood. Plead the cross. Sing of the precious name of Jesus. Recite the Scriptures and enforce the victory over the powers of darkness. Plead the blood over and over again. Agree with Christ triumphantly, '*It is finished*!' "[1]

Stretched Beyond My Comfort Zone

The message of this chapter was birthed during one of the times when I was being stretched far beyond my comfort zone.

Another seminar was coming and Jim turned to me and said, "Ann, I really feel like you're supposed to do a session." I felt totally inadequate. I said, "Oh Jim, I don't even know if I can come up with anything. I just feel too scattered."

Jim persisted, telling me, "I feel like this is something you need to do. It needs to be called, 'This Means War.' It's almost like I can see two generals in times past who were declaring a duel. They have taken off their white gloves with the long gauntlets attached, and they are slapping each other in the face as a formal insult, saying, 'This means war!' " When he said that, my mind went to the time Jim and I went to Haiti. Our oldest child, Justin, was two years old at the time. We prayed for a lot of people who were unable to have children, and I gave my testimony about our miracle child, Justin. At the same time, I firmly believed that God was going to give us other children too. I just knew it.

We didn't realize it at the time, but we later discerned that a trailing spirit of weakness and infirmity followed us back home from Haiti and waited for an opportunity to attach itself to me. I got pregnant with GraceAnn and immediately became extremely sick. From that point on, I had to battle that new enemy, the spirit of weakness and infirmity. The enemy didn't want me to be strong, and it was obvious. If I made a decision in the morning that I was going to go exercise and build up my strength and stamina, then I would get sick that afternoon.

I woke up one morning with a stiff neck, and I also woke up with the phrase, "*This means war!*" I thought, *I have got to go exercise. I don't care how much it hurts, I don't care how I feel afterward, I have got to go do this.* I had literally heard the enemy say, "You are so tired that you will never get well. You're so tired that you're not going to be able to exercise. I'm going to keep you in this tired place so you never, ever, get out of it." He wanted me to believe that I was helplessly trapped in his demonic cycle of weakness and infirmity.

That made me mad. Up to that point, I had always looked at the issue of exercise as a "personal discipline." But that day, I became thoroughly convinced that it was not just an issue of personal discipline—it was an issue of spiritual warfare. I had to guard myself. I had to put on my armor and make up my mind that by God's grace I was going to do this thing. I decided that even if I could only exercise one day a week, then I would consider it a victory because that was better than what I'd been able to do before.

Waging War With the Prophetic

My dear friend, Bonnie Chavda, delivered a word of the Lord over Jim and me concerning God's gift of strength and might to us. I took that word and believed it. I took hold of Paul's admonition to young Timothy: "This command I entrust to you, Timothy, my son, in accordance with the prophecies previously made concerning you, that by them you may fight the good fight" (1 Tim. 1:18).

For a period of months, on a daily basis, I would place my hands on my body and pray, "I come against the spirit of weakness and the spirit of infirmity in the name of Jesus. I call forth the spirit of strength and might to be in my body, to come upon my body, my soul, and my spirit, to be in every aspect of my being. And I stir up that spirit of strength in me." I began to feel stronger and stronger every day as I confessed the truth of that prophetic word over me. The only way I can describe it is that I felt like I was taking spiritual vitamins.

The most sure word of prophecy we can take into battle is the prophetic Word of God revealed in the Scriptures. It is time for us to band together, prepare our hearts, and gather our weapons of warfare. I don't know about you, but I'm saying, "Enough is enough! *This means war!*" I'm ready to strike out in the name of Jesus to reclaim the territory, rights, and blessings that are rightly mine in Christ Jesus. We should no longer tolerate the encroachment of the enemy in our families, our churches, or in our destiny as the Church of the living God. Let's band together and fight the good fight.

The Underestimated Power of Communion

We overcome the forces of darkness every time we join together in holy *communion*, the Lord's Supper. Communion is an act of warfare. I suspect that it is far more powerful than any of us can imagine; because every time we partake, we are proclaiming the Lord's death until He comes (see 1 Cor. 11:26). This is a marriage of our two great "weapons of mass destruction," the blood of the Lamb and our public testimony to the reality of Christ. What makes it even more powerful is the fact that the very act of sharing communion joins us together in the immeasurable power of unity in Christ!

I still remember how I felt a few years ago when I was battling an intense case of pneumonia that was so severe that I had been hospitalized for days. Two dear friends came to my hospital room and served me communion. I can't tell you the strength that came within me from that experience! It was wonderful. There is untold power in the Lord's Supper—communion.

One time when Jim and I were in one of our prayer group meetings, the Holy Spirit whispered to Jim, "The Lord's Supper is one of the most overlooked and highest forms of spiritual warfare." This so struck Jim that he wrote it down in the back of his Bible, and it is there yet to this day. When we take communion, we are publicly testifying what the blood of Jesus has done for us. It is awesome.

Another time when we had a prayer group retreat, as we were taking communion, the sky lit up with golden light, and rays of His Presence came upon us all! The celebration of the blood is one of the highest weapons of spiritual warfare. Through it we humble acknowledge our need and proclaim His vast supply. Oh, the blood of Jesus!

Pray this prayer with me before you do anything else. Bathe yourself in the cleansing protective flow of the blood the Lamb through the power of this prayer:

I declare what the Word says that the blood of Jesus does for me. Through the blood of Jesus, I am redeemed out of the hand of the devil. Through the blood of Jesus, all my sins are forgiven. The blood of Jesus Christ, God's Son, continually cleanses me from all sin. Through the blood of

Jesus, I am sanctified, made holy, and set apart to God. My body is a temple of the Holy Spirit, redeemed, and cleansed by the blood of Jesus Christ. Satan has no place in me; he has no power over me through the shed blood of Jesus Christ. Amen[2]

Endnotes

1. Jim Goll, "Fire on the Altar: Stoking the Flames of Revival Through Intercession," a training manual prepared for training intercessors (Nashville: Ministry to the Nations, 1995), 4.4.

2. From the teaching ministry of Derek Prince, Derek Prince Ministries, Charlotte, North Carolina.

Chapter 7

Treasures From the War Chest

Michal Ann Goll

I have also spoken to [you by] the prophets, and I have multiplied visions [for you] and [have appealed to you] through parables acted out by the prophets (Hosea 12:10 AMP).

Let me open up the Goll family war chest and pull out some treasures of God's faithfulness in supernatural encounters and divine provision. We each have various roles to play at different seasons in life. Most of these stories are from Jim's role in the field, joined with my prayers from the hidden place.

In November of 1986, Jim and I had just left the place of pastoral and campus ministry where we had been for 13 years. Our second child, GraceAnn, was born that December. Changes were the order of the day for the following January. We knew that God "had something up His sleeve," but we were still waiting for the details. Jim had just returned from a crusade in Haiti with our friend Mahesh Chavda and was waiting on the Lord in our little basement office when the Holy Spirit dropped this statement into his spirit: "I want to release *breakers* who will break open the way for New York City."

He decided to write a new friend in Bellingham, Washington, named Dick Simmons, whom he had just met on the missions trip to Haiti. In the letter he said, "The Lord seemed to be speaking something to me today about how He wants to 'release breakers' who will go before to break open the way for New York City." We didn't know much about Dick's background and history at that time, but the very day Jim wrote those words about "breakers," Dick was praying out of the Book of Micah and had found the verse that says, "The *breaker* goes up before them; they *break out*, pass through the gate, and go out by it. So their king goes on before them, and the Lord at their head" (Mic. 2:13).

One of Dick's greatest prayer burdens was for that great metroplex, as he had been ministering in and out of New York City for 30 years. We didn't know it, but he was literally praying, "Lord, where are Your *breakers* for New York City who will go before and open the way?"

Jim had never been to New York City in his life and wasn't really sure he should go there. He was thinking, *Why would a guy who grew up in a little town of 259 people (counting all the children and maybe some of the pets) want to go to some crazy town that ten million people call home?* Naturally, as soon as Dick Simmons received Jim's letter, he called our house and said, "Jim, I want to take you into New York City."

We didn't know it, but Dick had been David Wilkerson's first Teen Challenge director, and he had helped pioneer the first Teen Challenge facility in the world right there in New York City. We didn't know that he had attended the New York Bible Institute either, or that Pat and DeeDee Robertson had lived in the Simmons' house before they ever started the Christian Broadcasting Network in Virginia. All Jim knew was that this relatively new acquaintance (at the time) was saying, "I want to take you to New York City. I just feel like the Lord wants to do something."

A Word From a Seer

At the same exact time, our dear friend Bob Jones, a seasoned prophetic seer, had a dream. He had just been in New Orleans for a leadership conference where he ran into a man named Richard Glickstein, a Messianic Jew, who at the time pastored a church in Manhattan (in the heart of New York City). Once Bob got home, he had a dream in which he saw Jim and Richard Glickstein together *lying side by side in a bed.* (Just wait, there's obviously more to this....)

Bob Jones contacted Jim by phone and said he had received a vision in which he saw Jim lying in a bed with Richard Glickstein, and both of them had their eyes wide open. Jim interrupted Bob long enough to say, "I've never met anybody named Glickstein before." Bob just kept going. He said, "Yeah, but you guys were lying in bed together, and the Lord is going to make you intimate bedfellows and *watchers in the Spirit* together." Jim could only say, "Who knows, Bob? I don't know. We'll see."

While Jim was still thinking about Dick Simmons' invitation to New York City, Bob Jones had yet another vision. He saw a man whom he didn't recognize come and stand in front of him. Shortly after that, Bob was telling Jim on the phone, "I don't know who this man is, but the Lord described him to me. All I know, Jim, is that the Lord says you know who this man is." Then Bob began to talk about the man, saying, "The Lord says that this man is a general in the army of God, but he thinks that he's a private. The Lord says that this man has been wounded often by the Body of Christ, but he forgives daily. The Lord also says that He always delights to hear the prayers of this man." Then Bob began to describe to Jim how tall this man was, and what he looked like.

Jim immediately knew who Bob was talking about. He said, "Yeah, I know who that man is—that's Dick Simmons." Jim knew he had to make the trip to New York City, and when he met Dick there, he told him about Bob's visions. Dick took Jim on a preliminary tour of New York, beginning with the World Challenge Center, and they spent the night in prayer there. Then they stayed all night in a prayer room located in one of the upper floors of the Empire State Building. Jim told me, "We prayed all night, looking out of the windows at those colossal buildings, the ABC Television Network headquarters, and everything else. We were praying all night for God to invade those places with His glory."

The Vision Unfolds

The next day Jim and Dick Simmons decided, "Okay, let's go meet this Glickstein character—whoever he is." So they located the phone number for One Accord Fellowship, the congregation he pastored at the time, located near 6th Street in Manhattan. They had never met him before, but that day they met Richard at a restaurant. (Jim calls them "blind dates in the Spirit.") Richard was having lunch with John DeLorean, the man who designed the stainless steel sports car that many heralded as the "super car of the future." As Jim was sitting at the table with Dick Simmons, Richard Glickstein, and John DeLorean, he kept thinking, *God, why do I feel a little out of place here, yet at home at the same time?*

As soon as Jim had introduced himself to Richard, he turned around and introduced Richard to Dick Simmons. Bob Jones' vision was from the Lord because the Holy Spirit joined Jim together with Richard and they remain "intimate bedfellows in the Spirit of God" to this day, and they continue to work together as appointed "watchers in the Lord."

After that initial meeting, the Lord had Jim, Richard, Dick, and David Fitzpatrick, a pastor from Michigan and one of Richard's closest prayer buddies, meet together for intensive prayer every four to six weeks, with each prayer vigil lasting anywhere from three to seven days. They cried out to the Lord together like this over a period of 18 months or so. Much of that time was spent in the Ukrainian Pentecostal Church building in New York City, where Richard Glickstein's Fellowship met on Sunday evenings. The atmosphere in that place was unusual, according to Jim. It was almost as if there was an opening in the heavens over that location. Jim says of it, "There was in some way or another a grace that was there. I think the Pentecostal people from the Ukraine had paid a severe price for their faith, and they were longing for something special from Heaven."

During those times of consecrated prayer, the four men would go to the Pentecostal Church building because it was vacant during the day. There they would spend hours and hours crying out to God. They would remind God of His Word for hours on end, praying through the Scriptures and praying ceaselessly in the gift of tongues, and sometimes simply waiting before the Lord in quietness.

As the four men sought God week after week and day after day, the Lord began to knit them together in the Spirit. In Jim's words, "We built a history together before the throne of God." As they were to discover, the Lord had a very specific purpose for this. Dick Simmons told us, "It took Jesus three years to find three men who could agree with Him, and perhaps that only happened as He took them up to the mount of transfiguration."

A Dream of Wall Street

After Jim had gone through this process of building a shared history with these men, he had a dream about Wall Street, the famous financial center in the heart of Manhattan. Even though Jim had now been to New York City a number of times, he had never been to Wall Street before. His total knowledge of the appearance and activities that go on there were limited to what he had seen in television news footage about Wall Street.

Jim told me, "In this dream I saw a ticker tape clock, a digital kind of thing, and I saw the number 2600. Then I heard someone say, 'When Wall Street hits 2600, this is the demarcation. Count 40 days after.' I didn't know what to do with it, but during the dream, I could also see or feel the words, 'nervous frenzy.' " Jim wasn't sure what to do with the dream, but he thought it was interesting, filed it away, and occasionally would quiz the Holy Spirit and pray over the revelation.

There are many different, diverse anointings in intercession. Some have to do with governmental prayer burdens, some center on the nation of Israel and the Middle East, some concern prayers for those in authority, for revival, for families, etc. Then there are prophetic intercessory people who pick up the current burden of the Lord and pray out of the revelatory gifting. At times, Jim in particular has found himself praying as both a "crisis intercessor" and a prophetic intercessor. Although each of us has specialty graces, we also must make ourselves available to whatever the Lord needs at that moment.

It was August, and the men had already prayed for five hours at the Ukrainian church when they traveled to key spots in the city to "pray on site with insight." They had just prayed at Federation Hall, the place where George Washington was inaugurated as President. From there, they entered an Episcopal church building where George Washington went after his inauguration. History records that he rode his horse through the muddy streets to that church and knelt in prayer there to dedicate himself and the nation to the Lord.

The prayer team went to the same place and literally prayed the prayers of George Washington again. Jim said, "I prayed as I stood before God for our nation, that judgment could be withheld, and that mercy would be released." The men decided to return to Federation Hall, which was only two blocks or so away from Wall Street. At that point, Jim began to sense an inner stirring or urgency in his spirit and he said, "Listen, guys, all I know is that I had this dream that said, 'When Wall Street hits 2600'...." (Today we think it is nothing for Wall Street trading volume to hit 7800 or more, but a volume of 2600 was astronomical at that point in time because it had never gone that high before.)

Jim told his companions, "The dream said, '*When Wall Street hits 2600, this is a demarcation. Count 40 days after,*' then there were the words '*nervous frenzy.*' All I know is that I've got to go down there. I've got to check this thing out." So Dick Simmons and Richard Glickstein and another friend of Jim's named Kevin went with him, while David remained behind to cover them in prayer. Jim was amazed as he walked through all the museum-like sections of the Wall Street Stock Exchange building. They finally came to an enclosed glass mezzanine built like a balcony overlooking the trading floor—it was exactly like the scene Jim had seen in his dream.

There were between 50 and 75 people crowded into the enclosed balcony area, and they were from all over the world. Jim remembers that there were a lot of Japanese and other Asian people there, and people were speaking all kinds of different languages. There were head phones available along the balcony area offering translation services into a number of foreign languages for the many tourists. Meanwhile, Jim and the other prayer warriors with him were getting this mounting urgency that the Lord wanted to release something dealing with a wake-up call for the nation. One of the men began to pray for God to shake the place or something similar to that, but it just didn't seem like that was the direction God wanted them to go. Finally, Jim said, "Guys, all I know is that I had this dream, and I feel like I have something that I'm supposed to pray and release."

Hitting the Target

Jim faced the trading floor where trading was still going on at a furious pace as he closed his eyes (although his companions didn't know his eyes were closed until later). The other men quietly surrounded him and laid their hands on him and they began to pray in the Holy Spirit—even though there were police guards stationed in the mezzanine area. Jim became totally detached from everything around him as the men laid their hands on him. He began to pray in the gift of tongues while it seemed like the Lord prophetically placed a bow and arrow in his hands. He said, "I remember pulling the bow back while my eyes were still closed. Then a word came up out of me with unusual authority, '*I shoot the arrow into the heart of the god of mammon, and I command it to go deep, deep, deep!*' "

The moment Jim prayed, this arrow in the spirit flew to its mark. Just as quickly as he was clothed with the supernatural enduement, it also lifted after the engagement had occurred. Evidently, just before Jim released the "arrow" of the Spirit, he was praying in tongues at an extremely loud volume. (When Dick Simmons visited his friend, Pat Robertson, one time, he told him, "Pat, I've got to introduce you to a man who prays louder in tongues than I do.")

Jim's eyes were still closed, and he could tell that something seemed to happen when he launched the arrow of the Spirit toward the target. The other men didn't know that Jim's eyes were closed, and a couple of them were asking him, "Did you see *that*? Did you see that?"

Jim said, "What are you talking about?" They answered, "You mean you didn't see it?" Jim shook his head and said, "No, what are you talking about? I had my eyes closed."

As the men compared notes later, Jim and Richard Glickstein remember sensing that a supernatural authority had come upon them. Richard Glickstein remembers feeling as though God had put a javelin in his hand! He thrust his "javelin of the Spirit" at the same instant that Jim released the prayer arrow of the Spirit. Unlike Jim, Richard's eyes were wide open.

He saw what Jim didn't, and he quickly explained what had happened. Down on the trading floor, plainly visible from their location, was a large digital clock displaying the current time of day. It was used to signal the opening and closing of the trading day. At the very moment Jim had prayed his prayer and released the arrow of the Spirit, the face of the digital clock flipped to 1:26—only this clock also displayed seconds. So this digital clock on the Wall Street trading floor hit exactly "1:26.00" as Jim and the other men prayed. This brought to mind the word of the Lord: "When Wall Street hits 2600, this is a demarcation. Count 40 days after." Not only did the digital clock hit this mark from the dream, but the trading at Wall Street also reached the infamous mark of 2600 that day.

Exactly 40 days later, the stock market crashed 508 points in a single trading day, sending shock waves and a "nervous frenzy" throughout the United States and the world. We knew it was a mercy warning to our country. It was God's gentle warning to our country to wake up and get its financial house in order. A mercy warning came in those days. Have we listened? Are more shots on the way?

Another Pearl From the Chest

I've already shared how I had to deal with a spirit of infirmity that followed us home from a ministry trip to Haiti, but we have had many adventures in that incredible nation. I won't go into any of them in detail, but Haiti is a particularly difficult nation to minister in because of happenings early in that nation's history. As Jim mentioned in his book, *The Lost Art of Intercession*, Haiti was called "the pearl of the Antilles" in the 1800s, and Port Au Prince, the capital city, was supposedly named for the Prince of Peace. Evidently the Haitian people were so desperate to break free from France's grip that they dedicated the nation to the devil, hoping he would give them power to win independence. That freedom came, but Haiti became enslaved to the dark powers behind the voodoo religion.[1]

We dearly love the people of Haiti, and Jim has ministered in that country on 14 different occasions. Some of these trips were up-front work for an outdoor crusade with healing evangelist Mahesh Chavda. These meetings were powerful and were used to confront the powers of darkness. On one trip, after the fourth nightly meeting, there was an announcement made over the national radio station by those in opposition to the crusade. They proclaimed that the voodoo priests were going to meet at their normal location at the normal time that afternoon because their "kingdom was under siege." In turn, the team with Mahesh, Dick Simmons, and Jim rallied in prayer. Kingdoms were at war with one another.

That night the Holy Spirit moved among God's people in a raw and powerful manner that broke the power of the voodoo priests who were even trying to interrupt the crusade meetings. Halfway through the fifth night's meeting, a chain gang of witch doctors and the like came running through the outdoor crowd, trying to disrupt it. Jim stomped on the flatbed truck to send a message to the intercessors below it to pray harder. Intercession arose all the more!

God sent a whirlwind filled with dust that blew so hard it frightened the voodoo priests and their followers away! The opposition left and the crusade went on. That last night of the crusade, a 77-year-old woman who had been born blind was miraculously healed by the Lord Jesus Christ as Mahesh laid his hands upon her. Jim recalls how her testimony was heard throughout the Caribbean region over the airwaves as she lifted her hands to Heaven and shouted in Creole, "Praise the Lord!" Once she was blind, but now she saw. Yes, praise the Lord!

Intercession arose day and night those days the team was amassed in Haiti. What goes up must come down! Yes, prayer precedes supernatural encounters.

Justin's Angelic Visitation

Many of our most memorable encounters in the Spirit have taken place in our home. One time Jim was involved in a critical prayer vigil in Atlanta, Georgia, while we were living in the south Kansas City area. I was busy taking care of the house and the ministry and watching the kids at our little house on Herrick Street. Our oldest son, Justin, was about seven years old at the time, but he had an incredible experience in the Lord. He was sleeping on the top bunk of his bed when he opened his physical eyes and saw some "clouds" coming down into his room. When he looked up into the clouds, he could see a bright throne with four winged creatures around it. Then he saw a ladder come out of the clouds and down into his room.

He watched as angels came down the ladder one at a time carrying what looked like fire in their hands. The last angel placed a piece of stationery on his dresser and then went back up the ladder, which in turn went back up into the clouds. Once the clouds disappeared, Justin said he couldn't see the winged creatures or the throne anymore. Only the stationery remained behind, in the exact position where the angel had placed it.

Justin got up and came into my room and began to tell me what he had seen. He even drew a picture of the four creatures he'd seen. He told me that each of the creatures had four faces: one like an eagle, one like a lion, one like an ox, and one like a man—just like the angelic beings described in the Book of Revelation and the Book of Ezekiel! Justin also said that they had something like fish scales on them. I finally sat down with him and read key passages out of the Book of Revelation. When Justin heard the words "...four living creatures full of eyes..." (from Rev. 4:6), he said, "Oh, well, that's it."

Then Justin described the piece of stationery he said the angel had left behind. He said there were two angels up in each corner of the stationery, and in beautiful handwriting was written the short message, "Pray for your dad." I'll never forget that one in all my days. When I told Jim about it, he was amazed. He was amazed not only because his son had experienced a dramatic supernatural encounter with angels, but also because only the Lord could know how urgently Jim needed his son's prayers during that time. God's ear leans when children pray.

Prayer Precedes Supernatural Activity

Jim and I have seen again and again how angelic ministry is released in response to the prayers of God's people. Jim often speaks of our Czech friend, Pastor Evald Rucky, who, it appears, was taken up into Heaven while his body was in a three-day coma caused by a severe heart attack. Evald told Jim many amazing stories of the things he saw there, but one revelation in particular illustrates one of the ways God answers prayer through angelic intervention and visitation. Evald told Jim that while he was suspended between Heaven and earth, he saw dark clouds over central and eastern Europe that were being penetrated by white lights going up and down from the heavens. He asked, "What are these white lights?" The Holy Spirit explained to him, "These are My angels being released in answer to the prayers of the saints." Evald realized that they were breaking up the black clouds, which were territorial spirits massed over central and eastern Europe.[2]

Pastor Evald also told Jim that he saw a white bridge come up out of Ethiopia in North Africa and arch right through the clouds to come back down in Israel. Then he watched as thousands of black men and women walked over this white bridge from Ethiopia and stepped onto the soil of Israel. Perplexed by what he saw, Evald asked, "What is this?" The Holy Spirit said, "These are My ancient people—the Jews—returning to their homeland." Evald persisted, "How does this occur?" A response came, "Oh, this too happens in response to the prayers of the saints."

Shortly after Evald was miraculously returned to his body and totally healed, he and the rest of the world received the news about "Operation Solomon." News organizations around the world flashed the story of a massive airlift conducted by the IDF (Israeli Defense Force) in cooperation with the Jewish Agency, the Israeli Foreign Ministry, and other governmental bodies, including the government of Ethiopia. Aircraft airlifted 14,400 Ethiopian (Black) Jews from the deserts of North Africa to Israel within a 48-hour period. The airlift made history as these beleaguered Jews were returned to their ancestral homeland, Israel. The arrival of the Jewish refugees brought tears to many of the thousands of Israelis who took part in the re-unification of the Ethiopian Jews with their 20,000 family members already in Israel.

Operation Solomon made 40 separate flights to bring most of Ethiopia's Jews to Israel. These Ethiopian Jews sought a new life in the Jewish state that hopefully would be free of religious persecution. The airlift was the largest mass evacuation of "Diaspora Jews" that the nation of Israel has ever mounted in its then 43-year history, and some sources said it was reminiscent of the biblical exodus. Evald's hospital sickbed vision had been 100 percent accurate.

Restoring the Ancient Tools

In 1991, during a prayer retreat in Kansas, Jim had a visionary experience. As he prayed at the 2 a.m. watch, Jim saw a picture of "an ancient tool." He asked the Holy Spirit, "What is this?" and the Spirit said, "These are the ancient tools." When Jim asked what the ancient tools were, he was told, "The watch of the Lord. I will restore the ancient tools of the watch of the Lord. It has been used, and it will be used again to change the expression of Christianity across the face of the earth."

The term, "watch of the Lord," wasn't new to Jim or to me. He had heard the phrase used in connection with the rich history of the Moravian Church, which was founded by Czech Evangelical Brethren in the 1700s who were fleeing persecution for their faith. They left Moravia and Bohemia, two states of what is now the Czech Republic, and fled to an area called Saxony in what is modern East Germany today. The religious refugees were led by a man named Christian David, and they found refuge under the favor and protection of a powerful nobleman named Count von Zinzendorf, who was himself a devout Christian. The Moravians are especially remembered for maintaining a prayer watch of unbroken prayer, petition, and praise that lasted well beyond the 100-year mark. The prayer that they offered is credited by many with launching and fueling the great missionary movement that changed the world in the eighteenth century.

Jim offers a detailed description of our trip and prayer vigil at the original site of the Moravian settlement at Herrnhut in *The Lost Art of Intercession*. It was there that the Holy Spirit descended on our team of intercessors and imparted a wonderful and unforgettable anointing and burden for prayer.[3] That trip was marked by encounter after encounter with divine providence, provision, and power.

One of the most remarkable things we received from the Lord at Herrnhut was the prophetic sense that God was essentially birthing "a new Pentecost" by planting His holy fire in 120 cities around the world. Thousands of years ago, He launched the Church in the fires of Pentecost in Jerusalem by filling the 120 people in the upper room with the baptism of the Holy Spirit and with fire. That small fire ignited the whole known world and is even now sweeping across the nations of this earth. Then the Lord told us that He was setting the fire of prayer and His Presence in at least 120 cities around the world. These were places where the

Lord was going to release a full demonstration of "the house of prayer for all nations."

A Supernatural Guide

Richard, David, and Jim had another unusual experience in Minsk, Belarus, when they embarked on a "prayer assignment" in the heart of the Commonwealth of Independent States' capital at midnight. They, with a team of many others, had participated in Hear O Israel's International Festival of Jewish Worship and Dance. The successful outreach was now over and their prayer assignment could convene. Due to the nuclear fallout from the Chernobyl disaster, great damage was released in Belarus. Many people (children especially) had serious illnesses in the stomach and lungs that they called the Chernobyl disease. The Lord put it on the men's hearts to intercede concerning this. They found out through a meeting with government officials that there was fear that the radiation fallout was about to enter into the river that ran through the heart of the city.

The men felt they needed to pray some very specific prayers at a downtown site in Minsk where a large monument had been erected bearing a great red star, a symbol of the Communist party. The signs of Communism were all still in place, and in May of 1994, a Communist president was elected by Belarus. The Holy Spirit showed the team, through prophetic revelation, to go to the heart of the city, pray at this main Communist monument, and then symbolically throw branches into the river, praying for the waters to be healed.

Many of the subways were not operating that late at night. None of the men knew for sure how to get to the proper location, and it wasn't quite proper for Americans to ask how to reach a Communist monument at midnight. But they also knew that they were supposed to pray at that specific location. Jim stepped into the hotel elevator to meet his two intercessory friends in the lobby of the hotel. They didn't know how they were going to get to the place, and once they reached the general location, they wouldn't be assured of how to get back. It was late. Things didn't look too good. But the Lord was in charge.

Back at the hotel, when Jim's two friends stepped into the elevator, they were joined by a total stranger. As Richard and David walked out into the lobby to meet Jim, the Russian-looking stranger walked along with them. He even walked with them right into the subway station! They didn't think much of it at first. Then the man boarded the subway with them and told them where to get off and how to catch the next subway train connection. He rode along with them and again helped them catch the right connecting train to reach their designated location. How did this man know where they were going? They had not peeped a word to anyone.

The stranger stepped off the subway with Jim and his friends and actually escorted them to the underground entrance of the towering government monument. Then he walked them out of the subway, pointed, and said in English, "Now this is where you are to pray." He quickly walked back down the steps as Jim and his friends said, "A-h-h-h, yes." By the time Jim turned around in the tunnel to thank the guide for his help, the man was gone— nowhere to be seen. Jim says of that experience, "I think we had an angelic escort take us to our appointed place of prayer. God must have wanted our prayers that night!"

Did they pray at the monument? Did they find branches to throw in the nearby river? Well, of course! The outcome? We will let time determine the fruits of the prayers that they launched that night. Whatever the case, the men were definitely guided by a supernatural means that night.

An Invitation

What does all this have to do with you? Everything. Jim and I are ordinary people serving an extraordinary God—and so are you. We have experienced supernatural encounters because we made ourselves available to the Lord. He wants His house to be a house of prayer, and you and I are to seek Him individually with all our hearts. He longs to share times of quietness and solitude with us, and He wants to establish us as lights of His glory and pillars of His strength in times of storm. There is no better time to begin an adventure in prayer than right *now*, in Jesus' name.

> *Lord, I want to fill up the treasure chest of my life with testimonies of Your power, intervention, and great love. I agree with the Book of Daniel where it says, "The people that do know their God shall be strong, and do exploits." As I yield my life to You, do great and mighty things in and through my life. In Jesus' wonderful name. Amen.*

Endnotes

1. Jim W. Goll, *The Lost Art of Intercession* (Shippensburg, Pennsylvania: Revival Press, 1997), adapted from material on pages 53-54.

2. Goll, *The Lost Art of Intercession*, adapted from page 94.

3. Goll, *The Lost Art of Intercession*, see particularly Chapters 1 and 4.

Chapter 8

Prophetic Dreams

Michal Ann Goll

For God [does reveal His will; He] speaks not only once, but more than once, even though men do not regard it [including you, Job]. [One may hear God's voice] in a dream, in a vision of the night, when deep sleep falls on men while slumbering upon the bed. Then He opens the ears of men and seals their instruction [terrifying them with warnings] (Job 33:14-16 AMP).

Dreams have been called "the sleep language," and they have been used by God ever since the time of the creation to bring divine revelation to mortal men and women. Scripture even calls a prophet a "dreamer of dreams" (see Deut. 13:1; Num. 12:6).

I can tell you that the Lord has used dreams to communicate and minister to me in amazing ways. That is why I love to go back through some of my dream logs and remember how God has spoken and imparted things to me over the years. As we go through life day by day, these dreams and impartations often seem to be just little things compared to some of the more dramatic ways and visitations of God. But when we take the time to look back, we can see how much God has imparted and given to us. This can be a tremendous tool to reveal an awesome revelation of how much He loves us and cares about even the most minute parts of our lives.

The Lord has used dreams to bring healing to my emotions and focus to my personal ministry. It was through dreams that the Holy Spirit enhanced the ability to open my eyes of faith and see myself as God sees me. And it was through dreams that I received a deposit and first began to (and still do) carry the "burden of the Lord" in prophetic intercession and have compassion for others. Many people today with the Western worldview tend to dismiss dreams as foolish or even demonic. They just don't know what they are missing! So many people are totally dismissing God's opinion on the matter:

> *For these men are not drunk, as you suppose, for it is only the third hour of the day; but this is what was spoken of through the prophet Joel: "AND IT SHALL BE IN THE LAST DAYS," God says, "THAT I WILL POUR FORTH OF MY SPIRIT UPON ALL MANKIND; AND YOUR SONS AND YOUR DAUGHTERS SHALL PROPHESY, AND YOUR YOUNG MEN SHALL SEE VISIONS, AND YOUR OLD MEN SHALL DREAM DREAMS; EVEN UPON MY BONDSLAVES, BOTH MEN AND WOMEN, I WILL IN THOSE DAYS POUR FORTH OF MY SPIRIT and they shall prophesy* (Acts 2:15-18).

The whole realm of prophecy, prophetic dreams, and visions is openly supernatural, and for that reason is too quickly dismissed by many in this supposedly "logic and knowledge-driven" age. I can trace my "baptism" in the realm of dreams and revelation to April 7, 1991. I had a dream in which Jim and I were participating in a small church meeting. One man stood up and said prophetically, "There is a woman here whom God will give great boldness and speech and proclamation, one who is naturally very quiet and reserved."

Jim was sitting next to me, and he said, "I know who that is for. That's for Michal Ann Goll." Later on in my dream, a woman came up to me and told me of a "new life" that was in my body, which was confirmed by several women that night. God by His grace and loving kindness had overcome me, and He was continuing to overcome my natural reserve by placing a spirit of boldness and proclamation upon and within me.

When these prophetic words were given to me through my dream, I had a choice to make. I could reject the move of God in my life like my biblical namesake, Michal (my name is Michal Ann). Or, I could receive God's word and let Him *flow* through me as the true meaning of Michal implies. (*Michal* is a Hebrew word meaning "rivulet, stream, brook" or a flowing stream of water.) Michal was the first wife of David and the youngest daughter of King Saul. After her father's death, she rejected the move of God that prompted King David to dance without inhibition or hindrance before his people. She was so interested in preserving her royal station and keeping up a pretense of false respectability that she missed God by despising her anointed husband. As a result, she was barren and childless for the rest of her life. (See Second Samuel 6.) I refuse to follow in her footsteps.

I received the word of the Lord that day in 1991, and since then I have seen my name literally fulfilled by the grace of God. He has made me a "flowing stream of grace and favor." (*Ann* means "grace.") I do not want to be a mocker of God's Presence and thus be barren. I want to have many "children" in the spirit realm, in whatever way God wants to bring them into my life.

I've really tried to be careful and guard that. I know what it is like to walk through seven years of barrenness and then experience the healing power of God and bring four children into the world, despite the medical world's claims that it was impossible. He took me from a place of barrenness, and He gave me favor and grace, both in the natural and spiritual realms. Now He is allowing me to become a channel, a brook, or a stream of His glory so that I can give to others the things He has given to me.

Men and women need to realize that dreams are a lot like pregnancy and childbirth. When God speaks to you through a dream, or in one of His many other revelatory ways, you are carrying a baby in that dream. Like a mother in the natural, you don't know what that dream is actually going to look like when you finally see the finished product. You know that there is new life within you, but you don't know what that "baby" is going to look like, if it will be masculine or feminine, or if it will have blonde, black, brown, or red hair. You don't know if the "child" will be studious, intellectual, or athletic. All you know is that the life of God has somehow been deposited in you, and you love that life. Everything within you is committed to guarding and caring for that life within your spirit.

When God gives us dreams, we have no idea what the end result of those dreams will be. It is a lot like receiving a colt, a young horse, at random. You don't know what kind of horse you are getting, and you don't know what that horse is going to be like a few years down the road. It may be very regal and stately, or it may be a teeth-rattling bucking bronco! We don't know when God is going to give us directional dreams concerning our giftings and callings. What we *do know* is how to respond when a dream comes. Each of us needs to say:

> *Lord, I just want life. Whatever it looks like, however You decide to bring it into maturity, that's what I want. I want to ride the kind of horse that You have given me to ride. I want this dream to come to completion in the way that You have planned. I remove my hands from it and relinquish any effort to control it and figure it all out. Lord, I just want the dream to grow within me and come to full maturity, in Jesus' name.*

This has been the key to the whole realm of spiritual dreams and revelation for me. We don't know where we are going except that as we trust Him, we are to always be drawn closer to God. That should be the cry of our hearts for any dream experience or supernatural experience that we have. If it doesn't bring us closer to Jesus, if it doesn't help us to understand the work of the cross and become more firmly rooted in God's love, then we need to seriously question the validity and source of the experience.

The Two Categories of Dreams

Dreams tend to fall into two main categories: dreams of self-disclosure or internal dreams and dreams of outside events or exter*nal dreams*. Each of these broad categories includes a number of different sub-categories as well. Some of the following material has been adapted from the excellent prophetic teaching ministry of John Paul Jackson of Fort Worth, Texas.

Internal Dreams (or Self-Disclosure Dreams)

This category of includes at least nine different types of dreams common in the Christian experience.

1. *Healing dreams* tend to bring divine forgiveness and love to us, and they are often able to deliver God's healing balm in places and ways that no other method can. I shared in a previous chapter how God gave me a sweet dream about a white-haired older man, a father, who often spent time with me and told me in all purity that he longed to embrace me because he loved the fragrance of my hair. That was a healing dream that God gave to me to heal a very specific and personal area of hurt.

   My father didn't receive the nurture that he should have received while growing up. As a consequence, he really didn't know how to provide love and nurture for his own kids later in life. This shortcoming in my natural father could have been used by the enemy to distort my image of my heavenly Father, but God wouldn't allow it. My heavenly Father used a recurring dream to impart the love and nurture that I was so hungry for as a child. I confess that He is obviously still working on my insecurities, but God brought supernatural healing to me through those dreams. (I am happy to say that my natural father is a totally different man today as well. He is very loving and affirming. He almost cries every time we have to leave after we visit him, and he loves for us to visit him. I believe that this change has come in part because God healed me through prophetic dreams so I could extend grace and understanding to my dad. This helped him forgive himself and be released to learn how to freely express his love for others.)

2. Cleansing dreams are given to help us "shower off" the day-to-day effects of living in a fallen world. These dreams are especially helpful when we are exposed to unclean influences that we consider to be "dirty." The Holy Spirit wonderfully refreshes and cleanses us, at times, from impurities in our soul. These cleansing dreams are tools of sanctification.

3. *Calling dreams* usually involve a direct appeal from God concerning a revealed purpose, vocation, invitation, or anointing that He has for you. God uses these dreams to tell you or confirm to you what He wants you to do presently or in times to come. Calling dreams release guidance into our lives, and they promote the release of faith that encourages you that God can and wants to use you. These dreams should always be confirmed by other sources of divine communication, such as prophecy, an inward witness of peace to your spirit from the Spirit of God, and by God's Word revealed to you as a *rhema* or living word by the Holy Spirit. (Remember, God's revelatory word never conflicts with the principle of the written Word.)

I am eagerly anticipating the fulfillment of one calling dream I've had several times in my life. It concerns my calling to operate in a very powerful gift of the word of knowledge—especially as a ministry tool to unbelievers outside of church settings. I dreamed that I was in an empty parking lot when I received a word of knowledge from God telling me that there was a gang leader in one of the apartments above a garage. God gave me a very specific word for that man that cut him to the quick, and He gave me the courage to seek him out and deliver the word personally. As a result, this gang leader came to know the Lord. Then I got into a car and began talking to the man who was driving it. Again God gave me a very detailed word of knowledge that created a divine "entrance point" to his heart so God could come and meet him.

I long for the day when I will move and minister in that level of personal prophetic anointing, but I'm not there yet. It happens from time to time as God wills, but not very often. I am believing that some day God will move me out into that level of faith and ministry. Again, I'm not there yet. But when God gave me that calling dream, it planted divine seeds of hope and faith within me to believe that *God can do it* in me—and that He wants to!

4. *Warning dreams* are often sent to us to warn us not to do certain activities or pursue certain courses, decisions, or relationships. They often have to do with spiritual discernment, where God provides details about a situation, presence, or activity that otherwise are unavailable to us. The Lord speaks to us through warning dreams to alert us to hidden snares, schemes, and devices of the enemy; or to warn about "blind spots" in our own character or judgment. These types of dreams have been very valuable to Jim and I. We have been tipped off ahead of time to watch out for certain enemies that want to encroach. To be pre-warned enables you to be prepared and armed for battle.

5. *False dreams* are inspired by the enemy to sow confusion, unrest, unbelief, fear, and hopelessness. When we are trying to discern a specific situation, we can follow the Lord's admonition, "Ye shall know them by their fruits" (Mt. 7:16 KJV). Although the Lord may cause us to feel unsettled, convicted, or even shocked at times, He never removes the eternal and unchanging marks of His Presence: peace, love, and joy. There is always hope in the Presence of the Lord for His emissaries. There is always an atmosphere of despair and hopelessness lingering around the presence of the evil one. The best way to deal with a dream that you feel is false is to ask the Lord for discernment and understanding. He will quickly reveal

the unclean source of the dream and dispel its power to confuse you. Pray for the grace gift of discerning of spirits and a word of wisdom. They are greatly needed in a generation such as we have today.

6. *Body dreams* are dreams that are directly or indirectly influenced by the condition of your physical body. If you are sick and you have a dream about being sick, guess what? You are sick! If you are pregnant and you dream that you are pregnant, then guess what? You are pregnant. Sometimes we get so involved in what is going on with our physical bodies that those things find their way into our personal dream language. (Common sense is an indispensable discernment tool in the prophetic realm.) In other words, it is true that our natural state of affairs affects our screen at night.

7. *Exhortation dreams* are used by God to give us courage to continue on in our God-given tasks. They inspire us to be bold and to go forth in God's strength and power. One time Jim and I were getting ready to go to Vancouver, Washington, and I had been throwing up off and on all day long. Meanwhile, I was trying to get my kids ready to stay with their friends and pack myself besides. I would pack for 5 minutes and then have to lie down for 20 minutes, pack for 5 minutes, and lie down for 20 minutes. I was just feeling horrible! I was thinking, *Lord, how can I do this? We are going to have to get up at four or five in the morning, and we're staying up late anyway.* My stomach was hurting and I was feeling worse by the minute.

I woke up in the middle of the night and sensed an angelic presence at the doorway of the room. I could literally feel warmth on my body where the rays of light emanating from his form shimmered toward me. Somehow I knew that they were warm healing rays. I felt like I had just been through a long and dreary winter season and I was finally basking in the warm sunshine of the first really sunny warm day of spring. Up until the moment the angelic figure appeared, I had felt "chilled to the bone." When I glanced at the clock, it said 1:11 a.m. I knew that God often speaks through the numbers that appear in our dreams, and I wondered what it meant. Just before I went back to sleep, I said, "Lord, what is 1:11?"

After quizzing the Holy Spirit, I slipped into another dream in which I found Mike Bickle, the senior pastor of Metro Christian Fellowship in Kansas City, Missouri. I said, "Mike, I just had this experience, and the clock said 1:11. Can you tell me what it means?" Mike had a really thin Bible in this dream (because it only contained the Books of Colossians, Ephesians, and Philippians). Mike said, "Oh, that is Colossians 1:11." I then awakened and found my Bible, and the passage where it says, "[We pray that you will be] strengthened with all power, according to His glorious might, for the attaining of all steadfastness and patience; joyously giving thanks to the Father..." (Col. 1:11-12). That was exactly what was happening to me. The angel was giving me strength to continue on. God strengthened, confirmed, and established me, once again, through a dream in the night season.

8. Warfare dreams are literally God-anointed and God-ordained engagements against powers of darkness while you are still sleeping. Even when our bodies are sleeping, the Holy Spirit within us is awake and vigilant. That is why God can speak to you while you are in a deep sleep. This also explains how God can call and anoint you to actually do things in the "spirit realm" while you are sleeping. Remember, God never sleeps nor slumbers, and He gives to His beloved in their sleep (see Ps. 121:4; 127:2). Perhaps, at times, the Holy Spirit engages in battle while you are sleeping. Great! Fight on, O Mighty Warrior.

External Dreams (or Dreams of Outside Events)

This is the second major category of dreams, with the following characteristics:

1. They are concerned with *outside events* involving the world, the church, our family, or our friends.

2. This is a specialized category. Some dream analysts tell us that this dream category will only account for approximately five percent of our total dream activity. (This varies, though, according to your spiritual gift mix.)

3. These dreams are usually given to *tell us to pray.* They seem to be God's way of providing "insider information" for the purposes of *private prayer* rather than public discussion with others. In some cases, God gives us interpretations of these dreams, but whether we receive an interpretation or not, it is still best to say little and just pray. This applies even if a name or a face is attached to the dream. In almost every case, the primary reason the Lord is bringing that person to your attention is so you can *pray on his or her behalf.*

4. Some *prophetically gifted people receive more of these dreams* about external events and people than any other kind. Again, this often seems to be given for purposes of prophetic intercession under the guidance of the Holy Spirit. (Note: This normally occurs only after God has given these prophetic individuals many internal or self-disclosure dreams and has worked all kinds of negative or hurtful things out of their lives. In some cases this may simply be a sovereign gift that God has placed in a person to serve the Body of Christ in this area. In this case, this person would be operating in a true "seer gift" and would thus receive a comparatively high percentage of external dreams about world affairs, events, Church situations, national events, economic events and warnings, and natural and spiritual catastrophes.)

Dreams are often confused with visions, and for good reason. The two are very closely related. Dreams are typically symbolic, while visions can often be more literal in their interpretation. We will look more closely at visions in the next chapter.

Log Your Dreams

I strongly encourage you to log or journal your dreams. We've learned through our studies, our own experience, and in sharing with other people who are well-versed in the area of dreams, visions, and the prophetic realm in general, that as you seek God, He will often create a unique dream language that will be reserved for you and God. That is because we don't serve a "cookie-cutter" God. He longs to have a unique and individual relationship with each one of us, and He will often speak to us using symbols or memories from our individual past or private thoughts known only to Him and to us. He will teach each of us our spiritual alphabet over a period of time and logging dreams is one of these teaching tools.

For example, a majority of the dreams that God has given me contained visual, mental, and even sensory images from the farmhouse where I was raised. Although my father struggled with his expression of affection in those years, I still have very warm and wonderful memories of my years at that farmhouse. I remember all our cousins getting together and I remember the times we would gather in the summer. We were just poor country people, but we still knew how to have fun. We used to spread out an old black tarp in the front yard, run water over it with a water hose, and then slide across the yard on our own homemade "slip and slide" system. We used to sleep outside along with all our little kittens, cats, and dogs in one wiggly, cuddly pile. Our relatives used to fill up our kitchen and sip coffee by the hour as they laughed and joked together. And every fall we would have a traditional family hayride and wiener roast with all my dad's relatives, sing songs, and enjoy life!

When I think of the family farmhouse, I think of all those warm memories and am reminded that it always represented a warm, loving, and safe place to me. So when I began to get a number of dreams involving the farmhouse, Jim helped me realize that

God was speaking of "the Father's house." These images of my natural father's house were symbolic of my heavenly Father's house. So I've learned that when something happens in the farmhouse of my dreams, it generally has something to do with the Body of Christ, with the Church, with the Father's house, and the house of believers. This is part of the unique language that God uses to speak to me, and is a great tool for interpreting. However, *if I had not logged it*, I may have never understood that key factor.

A Word of Wisdom

My final word on dreams comes from Ecclesiastics 5:7: "For in many dreams and in many words there is emptiness...." Although God gives us dreams for specific purposes and reasons, He also has given us a "more sure word of prophecy" in the Bible (see 2 Pet. 1:10). Life consists of much more than dreams. God is warning us not to base our lives or decisions on dreams alone.

You can't live in dreams, as wonderful as they may appear to be. If your study and experience of dreams is all you are doing, then you are missing the perfect will of God. Seek the Giver of dreams first, and everything else in your life—including your spiritual dreams—will fall into their proper place and order. Oh, I love the revelatory and supernatural ways of God! But I am not addicted to them as my sole means of supply, encouragement, and life. Thank the Lord, I have His sure word of prophecy—the Bible—that I can turn to every day. I am so grateful for dreams, but I do not seek for gifts; I seek the Giver and Creator!

> *Father, I need and desire these revelatory ways in my life. I desire both the spirit of wisdom and revelation of You, Lord Jesus. Counsel me in the night with prophetic dreams. Raise up Your Josephs and Daniels for our day. Pour out Your prophetic presence on this generation and fulfill the promises of Joel of old for the honor of Your great name. Amen.*

Chapter 9

Interpreting Dreams, Revelations, and Super-natural Encounters

Jim W. Goll

And they said to him, We have dreamed dreams, and there is no one to interpret them. And Joseph said to them, Do not interpretations belong to God? Tell me [your dreams], I pray (Genesis 40:8 AMP).

"Albert Einstein was asked where his theory of relativity had originated. He attributed it to a dream experience that he had in his youth. According to the story, he was riding in a sled which started going faster and faster until it approached the speed of light at which time the stars broke into fantastic colors. He said that the rest of his life was given to the meditation of that dream."[1]

This chapter is my attempt to compress many years of personal reading, study, prayer, as well as the things I've gleaned from the ministries of anointed people around the world into a few short pages. Let me begin with a short excerpt from a marvelous book by Herman Riffel entitled, *Dream Interpretation*:

> "General George Patton received intuitive military guidance from dreams. Robert Louis Stevenson wrote his book *The Strange Case of Dr. Jekyll and Mr. Hyde* from a dream. Dmitri Mendelev developed the periodic table of elements from one of his dreams. Niels Bohr received a Nobel prize for his quantum theory, which he claimed came from a dream. Friedrich Kekule received insight on the structure of benzene from the image of a snake biting its tail in one of his dreams. Elias Howe had a nightmare that gave him an idea by which he invented the sewing machine."[2]

God gives us dreams and revelations to help empower us to do the works of Christ. Yet they also reveal a creative aspect of God's nature. In a sense, the Lord takes some of the divine creativity resident in His limitless mind and heart and gently "blows" or breathes it into us. (This is actually a pretty good definition of the word *inspiration*.) This process births new concepts and ideas in our inner man upon which we begin to meditate consciously and unconsciously. Revelation is God's cradle of creativity whereby He shares with us His life-giving thoughts, plans, holy motivations, and aspirations.

The Nine General Forms of Revelation

There are several means or channels in which God delivers this revelatory grace. The following is a list of nine of these biblical avenues.

1. Scripture

2. Visions

3. Dreams

4. Trances

5. Visitations

6. Translations

7. Verbal Communication

8. Physical Sensations

9. Inner Witness

Illumination and Inspiration

There are two forms of revelation that come from reading the Word of God: *illumination* and *inspiration*. Revelation by illumination occurs when you are reading or meditating on a Scripture and you receive understanding from the Holy Spirit about that passage. It is involved more with inner understanding than with personal application. This also occurs when the Spirit of God brings to your mind a Scripture passage that applies to an experience or event. This is what happened to Peter in Acts 2:16, when he rose on the Day of Pentecost to calm the crowd in Jerusalem. He had just seen the violent wind rush through the upper room. Burned into his memory were the tongues of fire that rested on the 120 prayer warriors as the gift of the Holy Spirit was poured out upon them. As Peter stood up, the Holy Spirit *illuminated* Joel's ancient prophecy concerning the latter day when God would pour out His Spirit on all flesh, and Peter quoted it to the masses (see Joel 2:28-32). Spiritual illumination is marked by what some describe as the "ah-ha!" moment. It is the point when your mental and spiritual "light bulb" goes on.

Revelation by *inspiration* is even more personal than illumination. This type of revelation comes when an individual is reading or meditating upon the Word of God and the verse just seems to leap off the page! He or she realizes that this verse isn't simply a historical statement or wise nugget; it is a current, living Word from the living God for him or her. Inspiration is when God "breathes" an eternal truth into your deepest being, sparking new flames of divine hope, faith, and love. It is what some people call a *rhema*, the Greek term for "the spoken word."

It was important for us to cover these two premiere sources of divine revelation before we begin to talk about the heady things of dreams, visions, and supernatural encounters. Supernatural revelation is wonderful, but God wants us to get the bulk of our spiritual food, guidance, counsel, and instruction from His "more sure word of prophecy," the Bible (see 2 Pet. 1:19). Meditate on it. Eat it. Devour it. Read it. Sleep it. Listen to the Word of God spoken on tape. Get it deep inside of you. Store up the written Word within you so that the Spirit of God will have something to work with when He blows upon you.

> **The true revelatory "word of the Lord"**
> **does not compete with, but rather complements,**
> **the inspired Word of God, the Bible.**

Dr. David Yonggi Cho has stated, "The language of the Holy Spirit is dreams and visions," and the late Watchman Nee said, "The picture is the Holy Spirit's memory." As we mentioned in the previous chapter, dreams have been called "the sleep language" of God. Most people dream at least one hour per night, which adds up to just over 2.9 years of dreaming in a 70-year life span! The problem is that, after a dream, many of us don't remember what happened. We know that we go through certain sleep cycles, and we also know that there is a point in that cycle somewhere between a deep sleep and our wakened state when we have most of our dreams.

Why Visions and Dreams?

Many people question why God would give us visions and dreams when we have the Bible. Other than the obvious and very true answer, "Because He wants to," I believe that we could also say it is because it takes faith, discernment, and the constant help of the Holy Spirit to hear God's voice through these means. Besides that, their supernatural nature makes it impossible for man to take the credit for God's work when a dream or vision is proven to be true. These revelatory ways let God be God—and man be man. They are great lessons in pride and humility.

We need to hear the current, fresh voice of God today because I believe that there are two *constants* in His Kingdom:

1.   God does not change.

2.   He calls us to *constantly change*.

In a very real sense, you and I are in constant transition or movement from one level, stage, or place to another. We go from glory to glory. God is at work to conform us into His image. A mark of a maturing Christian is change. One of the first marks of backsliding is stagnancy! Let God invade your unholy comfort zones and change you into the image of His radical Son. Let His Spirit draw near and use whatever means He wants to get His job done. Perhaps He has a plan to prick your rigidity and make you the answer to your prayers. Therefore, let His fresh voice of His wooing presence be released in your life and twist your arm, if need be, into believing that Jesus Christ is the same yesterday, today, and forever tomorrow.

Visions While Awake and Asleep

In the previous chapter, Michal Ann described ten different kinds of dreams grouped under the two categories of internal dreams (dreams of self-disclosure) and external dreams (dreams of outside events). As she noted, visions are closely related to dreams, the difference being that dreams are typically *symbolic*, while visions can be more *literal* in their interpretation. Visions generally fall under two similar categories—*internal visions*[3] seen with the inner eye (while our eyes are closed); and *external visions* seen with the physical eyes wide open. Daniel had internal visions at night within his mind (see Dan. 4:5,10,13; 7:7). He also had external visions, which are recorded in Daniel 8:3 and 10:7. Paul the apostle received an internal vision when an angel spoke to him in a vision (see Acts 16:9).

Elisha's servant had an external vision when his eyes were opened so he could see the angelic armies of God with his physical eyes (see 2 Kings 6:17). Ezekiel had an open vision of Heaven and the throne of God with his physical eyes (see Ezek. 1:1). The

Old Testament prophets varied considerably in the number and degree of the visions they received. Zechariah, Jeremiah, and Amos had only a few visions while Daniel, Ezekiel, and Isaiah had many. It is very important to note that principle because we can get into erroneous comparisons when we say, "Well, I am only prophetic if I have visions." That is not the case. Join the crowd of "Jeremiahs." He is commonly called "the weeping prophet," although he wasn't very prolific in visionary revelation. He had a job to do and a unique set of gifts and skills with which to accomplish it. I think most of us would have to admit that Jeremiah did all right.

The Symbols of Dreams and Visions

In 1989, I was asleep when I saw a vision (an internal vision) in our bedroom of a white elephant that appeared to be made of clouds. The elephant started to come in upon me, and the closer it got the more I began to feel pressure, torment, and fear. It seemed like it just wanted to stomp me to death. My spirit man was wide awake, but I couldn't seem to wake up my body to fight against this thing. I found myself wrestling, trying to "awaken myself." I could hear myself struggling between sleep and the desire to re-buke this intruder. I was half snoring and half congested, making what appeared to me to be loud noises.

In reality, all my struggling woke up my wife and she gave me one of those proverbial midnight elbows. That made me *really* wake up, and I instinctively shouted, "Jesus." As soon as I got that holy name out of my mouth, I saw the power that was coming against me just break up and dissipate into thin air. I concluded that my encounter with this frightening creature was a gentle warning from the Lord of something that was coming that could end up in an intense encounter of spiritual warfare. The Holy Spirit wanted to tip us off ahead of time. I was glad He did.

Since dreams, visions, and revelations are full of symbolism, they need to be viewed much the same as parables. The first thing to do is *ask the Lord* to show you the central issue. When dreams, visions, or revelations are broken down into too many details, the meaning becomes increasingly obscure. What is the main, central issue He is trying to communicate? For me, and the experience I just mentioned, it was to prepare; an enemy was coming!

Three Realms for Interpretation of Symbols[4]

1. The first place to look for clues for interpretation is in Scripture. The Bible is full of parables and allegories from which to draw types, shadows, and symbols. Examples include the mustard seed being faith; incense being the prayers of the saints; seed representing the "Word of God"; and the candlesticks being local, city-wide, or regional churches.

2. Dream symbols are often colloquial expressions that fill our memory bank. They are turned into pictorial language by the Holy Spirit. God takes the "sayings" and idioms and uses them to speak spiritual truth. (An example is Gideon in Judges 7:9-15, where a barley loaf appears. Gideon grew up as a thresher of wheat and barley.)

3. The third realm of symbols comes from our own personal revelatory alphabet. In this case, the object or symbol does not necessarily mean the same to you as it would to others, such as:

   a. The meaning of animals. Consider the following:

   - Isaiah the prophet pictured the Messiah as a *lamb* led to the slaughter.

   - John's Gospel portrays Jesus as a shepherd and His disciples as little *lambs.*

   - The Book of Revelation pictures the *sacrificed lamb* as a Conqueror right *now.*
     Each time a "lamb" is used in these examples, it is in a different manner. Flexibility is the rule in proper interpretation.

   b. People who appear in our dreams may be seen in a literal sense, a symbolic sense, or according to the actual meaning of their name. (Ask yourself, "What does this person represent to me? What is the outstanding characteristic of the individual? What is the meaning of that person's name?")

c. Birth and death. This may be literal, figurative of something else, or spiritual, speaking of a new beginning. Thank the Lord that not all pregnancy dreams are literal! Oftentimes, birth and death dreams are symbols of a season we are headed into in our spiritual journey.

d. Children's dreams. This alone is a vast subject. Consider nightmares. How do you respond? Well, prayer, of course! At times you must look below the surface and detect the source of the nightmare. Perhaps tenderness is needed. (Remember, perfect love casts out fear.) But at other times, the prayers of rebuking an evil power is necessary. Many children also receive profound revelatory dreams depicting God's call on their lives. You are never too young to hear His voice. After all, remember the example of Samuel.

e. Sexual dreams may come to cleanse the defilement from flesh and spirit, to portray a call into intimacy, or to reveal natural desire and passion as part of the ordinary issues of human life. Some of these are showing the need to repent; others for greater cleansing. But at times, these peculiar dreams must only be interpreted symbolically as a call to greater union with Christ.

Recurring Symbols in the Bible

I've listed a number of recurring biblical symbols and colors adapted from Kevin Conner's excellent book entitled, *Interpreting Symbols and Types.*[5] When interpreting dreams, visions, and revelations, we must learn to take our interpretations first from Scripture, and then from our own lives. God is consistent with His symbolic language. How He spoke in the Book of Genesis will be similar to the symbols and types in the Book of Revelation. This holds true in our own life as well.

Classification of Symbols

1. Symbolic *actions* (Eph. 2:6; Ps. 10:1; Heb. 10:11-12)

2. Symbolic *colors* (Rev. 3:4-5; 6:2-6; 19:8)

3. Symbolic *creatures* (Rev. 12:9; Gen. 3:14; Lk. 13:31-32)

4. Symbolic *directions* (Lk. 10:15,30; Gen. 12:10–13:1; Jer. 1:14)

5. Symbolic *names* (1 Sam. 25:25; Jn. 1:41-42)

6. Symbolic *numbers* (Lk. 10:1; 2 Cor. 13:1; Deut. 19:15)

7. Symbolic *objects* (Mt. 16:18; Ps. 18:2; 1 Cor. 10:4)

Symbolic Colors

1. Amber—the glory of God (Ezek. 1:4; 8:2 KJV)

2. Black—sin, death, and famine (Lam. 4:8; Rev. 6:5; Jer. 8:21 KJV)

3. Blue—Heaven, Holy Spirit (Num. 15:38)

4. Crimson/Scarlet—blood atonement, sacrifice (Is. 1:18; Lev. 14:52; Josh. 2:18,21)

5. Purple—kingship, royalty (Jn. 19:2; Judg. 8:26)

6. Red—bloodshed, war (Rev. 6:4; 12:3; 2 Kings 3:22)

7. White—purity, light, righteousness (Rev. 6:2; 7:9; 19:8 KJV)

Basic Principles of Interpreting Numbers

If the student follows these principles, he or she will be preserved from error and extreme.

1. The simple numbers of 1-13 often have spiritual significance.

2. Multiples of these numbers, or doubling or tripling, carry basically the same meaning, only they intensify the truth.

3. The first use of the number in Scripture generally conveys its spiritual meaning.

4. Keep consistency of interpretation. God is consistent, and what a number means in Genesis, it means through all Scripture to Revelation.

5. The spiritual significance is not always stated, but may be veiled or hidden, or seen by comparison with other Scriptures.

6. Generally there is good and evil, true and counterfeit, and godly and satanic aspects in numbers.

Individual Numbers and Their Symbolic Meaning

1. One—God, beginning, source (Gen. 1:1; Mk. 6:33)

2. Two—witness, testimony (Jn. 8:17; Mt. 18:16; Deut. 17:6)

3. Three—Godhead, divine completeness (Ezek. 14:14-18; Dan. 3:23-24)

4. Four—earth, creation, winds, seasons (Gen. 2:10; Mk. 16:15; 1 Cor. 15:39)

5. Five—cross, grace, atonement (Gen. 1:20-23; Lev. 1:5; Eph. 4:11)

6. Six— man, beast, satan (Gen. 1:26-31; 1 Sam. 17:4-7; Num. 35:15)

7. Seven—perfection, completeness (Heb. 6:1-2; Jude 14; Josh. 6)

8. Eight—new beginning (Gen. 17; 1 Pet. 3:20; 2 Pet. 3:8)

9. Nine— finality, fullness (Mt. 27:45; Gen. 7:1-2; Gal. 5:22-23; 1 Cor. 12:1-12)

10. Ten—law, government (Gen. 1; Dan. 2; Ex. 34:28)

11. Eleven—disorganization, lawlessness, antichrist (Dan. 7:24; Gen. 32:22)

12. Twelve—divine government, apostolic fullness (Ex. 28:21; Mt. 10:2-5; Lev. 24:5-6)

13. Thirteen—rebellion, backsliding, apostasy (Gen. 14:4; 10:10; 1 Kings 11:6)

(Note: If you would like more information on biblical symbols, refer to Kevin Conner's book, *Interpreting the Symbols and Types*.)

Tips for Interpreting Dreams, Visions, and Revelations

1. Most of all, *dreams* should be interpreted on a personal basis first (see Jn. 10:3).

2. Most dreams, unlike many visions, should not be taken literally. They need to be interpreted (see Dan. 1:17; Gen. 40:8).

3. God will often use familiar terms you know (see Mt. 4:19).

4. Ponder on the dream or revelation and *ask the Holy Spirit* for insight (see Dan. 7:8; 8:15-16; Lk. 2:19; 1 Cor. 2:10-12).

5. Ask the Holy Spirit what certain thought, word, or issue is in the revelation. Reduce the dream to its simplest form. What is the main thought? What object or thought occurs most often? Frame it out like a giant jigsaw puzzle. Once you get the frame, the rest of it will fit together. What is the central *rhema* word? (Remember, not all the details are necessarily important or have meaning.)

6. Search it out in the Word. Dreams from the Lord will *never* go against His Word (see Prov. 25:2).

7. What did you sense and feel from the dream, vision, or revelation? Was it a good or evil presence? Did you sense fear, love, concern, hopelessness, or disappointment? What was the primary emotion? The type of emotion present will help determine proper understanding of the symbols.

8. Relate the dream to your circumstances.

9. Consecutive dreams often have the same or similar meaning (see Gen. 41:1-7,25-31). God will speak the same message more than once, but in more than one way.

10. What are the colors? Is everything black and white with only one main object in color?

11. Interpretations can be on three levels:

    a. Personal

    b. Church

    • local congregation

    • citywide church

    • church in a nation

    • global Body of Christ

    c. National and international (these can be governmental in nature)

12. More than one interpretation can come forth from one dream. Just as with Scripture, there is the historical or future context as well as the personal, present implication. So it is with dreams, visions, and revelations. It might be a general word for your church with specific applications for yourself (or others).

13. Some dreams may be understood only in the future. They unfold over time.

14. Write down in a journal the summary of your dream, vision, or revelation. Date it; note where you were and the time it occurred, plus the main emotions and a possible interpretation.

15. The key is *question, question, question*. Ask the Holy Spirit questions. The God who gave the revelation is

quite capable of giving you the understanding of the revelatory experience. Humility is marked by teachableness. Ask questions. Be teachable.

16. Walk with others! One key is this: God does not give everything to one person. Seek counsel and pray for input from others. God will supply many times through others.

The Three-Step Process

Often we have heard it said that there are at least three steps necessary in working with these prophetic ways: revelation, interpretation, and application. If you get your revelation right and miss it on your interpretation, your application is sure to lead you astray! You can even get the right discernment and interpretation to the revelation, but lack the wisdom ways of God for the application of Church or Kingdom life. Lord, help us!

Oftentimes, I feel that the Lord has purposefully left some blank spaces with each of us. Did you ever get just enough to get you motivated to do something for God's sake, and then you don't exactly know where to start? This is purposeful on His part! Why, you ask? He likes to be in charge!

There are two main issues here. First of all, God always leaves enough unknown issues involved so that we will not be dependent on ourselves, our giftings, etc. He wants us dependent on Him! This causes us to keep coming back and asking, "What did You say?" This process is called "relationship." God is more concerned about having a relationship with His children than He is in just being our knowledge dispenser. Second, God always leaves enough blank spaces in the equation because He is not looking for robots; He desires people of faith. If we knew everything, then we wouldn't need faith. Faith fills in many of the blanks. "Be it done to you according to your faith" is a statement that Jesus speaks to each one of us (see Mt. 9:29). Being prophetic does not mean that you know every step of everything you need to do beforehand! We are to be a prophetic people of faith walking in the footsteps of our father Abraham, "going out, and not knowing where you are going" (see Heb. 11:8).

Interpretations belong to God. Ask Him for them. Walk with others. Seek the Lord and He will give you the spirit of *wisdom* and *revelation* in this glorious man Christ Jesus. But remember, not everything that comes across the plate of your mind is from Him. I think I just heard you groan, "Uh oh, you mean there is more than just proper interpretation to our revelation in order to get the right application?" You bet! We are called to "test the spirits to see if they be of God" (see 1 Jn. 4:1). We'll get into that topic next!

Give to me the spirit of living understanding that I might know the wisdom ways of God in interpreting revelation. Teach me Your ways, O God, and lead me in the paths of righteousness. Grant me illumination from Your written Word, the Bible. Make it come alive to me, Holy Spirit. Grant grace to me as I humble myself in Your Presence this very hour. For the glory of Christ's name, I pray. Amen.

Endnotes

1. Jeremy Taylor, *Dream Work* (Mahway, New Jersey: Paulist Press, 1983), 7, as quoted by Herman Riffel in his book, *Dream Interpretation* (Shippensburg, Pennsylvania: Destiny Image Publishers, Inc., 1993), 1.

2. Morton Kelsey, *God Dreams and Revelation* (Minneapolis, Minnesota: Augsburg, 1991), as quoted by Herman Riffel in *Dream Interpretation*, 2.

3. Adapted from James Ryle's *Hearing the Voice of God* (Seminar Notes) (Boulder, Colorado: Boulder Valley Vineyard, 1992), 67.

4. Adapted from Ryle, *Hearing the Voice of God*, 65.

5. Kevin J. Conner, *Interpreting the Symbols and Types* (Portland, Oregon: Bible Temple Publishing, 1980).

Chapter 10

Wisely Judging Revelation

Jim W. Goll

Now a thing was secretly brought to me, and my ear received a whisper of it. In thoughts from the visions of the night, when deep sleep falls on men, fear came upon me and trembling, which made all my bones shake. Then a spirit passed before my face; the hair of my flesh stood up! [The spirit] stood still, but I could not discern the appearance of it... (Job 4:12-16 AMP).

What would you think if you had a spiritual experience that made your hair stand on end? Would you write it off as absolutely satanic or "off the wall" because it didn't fit your theological code? Many people would, and they would obviously be wrong in this case! This Scripture passage from the Book of Job was quoted in the first chapter to help describe the way Michal Ann and I felt when the angelic visitations began, and we chose it because it is amazingly accurate. Many people have supernatural encounters—are we to assume that they all come from the one true God or can there be other sources? How can we tell the source or nature of the spirit beings we encounter? What are the marks of a truly God-initiated encounter or revelatory experience?

There is only one dependable, unshakable guide through the minefield of supernatural encounters. In a world filled with spiritual voices of every type and description, Christians need to know how to make their way through a spiritual field littered with hidden (and deadly) weapons of the enemy designed to wound or destroy the unwary and the undiscerning.

Entire segments of the Body of Christ have "written off" the supernatural aspects of God's Kingdom and His workings in the Church because of fears about being deceived and led astray. Yet God *does speak* to His people today, and He is very capable of preserving us from harm and deception.

[Jesus said] *For everyone who asks, receives; and he who seeks, finds; and to him who knocks, it shall be opened. Now suppose one of you fathers is asked by his son for a fish; he will not give him a snake instead of a fish, will he? Or if he is asked for an egg, he will not give him a scorpion, will he? If you then, being evil, know how to give good gifts to your children, how much more shall your heavenly Father give the Holy Spirit to those who ask Him?* (Luke 11:10-13)

Now what do you think—can you trust your Father? I want to lay a clear, simple point here to begin. God wants you to hear His voice more than you want to hear it! He is a gracious Father who gives good gifts to His children. What is the foundation that must be laid? Stick close to Jesus. Seek Him. Love Him! Give your all to Him. James 4:8a says it this way: "Draw near to God and He will draw near to you." It can never be overemphasized: Cultivate intimacy with God through a relationship with His only Son, Jesus Christ.

You can trust your Father. If you ask Him for the things of the Holy Spirit in the name of Christ, you will get the real thing, not a counterfeit. But, nonetheless, there are many issues that we must consider when approching this valuable subject of wisely judging revelation.

Judging Revelation

God still speaks today through many different avenues, including visions, dreams, "inner knowings," His inner voice as well as His external audible voice, journaling, through His creation, etc. Yet our most important source of revelation is the *logos* canon of Scripture. The only way we can accurately and safely interpret supernatural revelation of *any kind* is to ask God for the spirit of wisdom and understanding, and to seek the counsel of the Lord.

Since the Bible is our absolute standard against which we must test *all* spiritual experiences, it should be obvious that we need to know and study God's Word. It is our only absolute, infallible, unchanging standard of truth. Just as you must learn to crawl before you learn to walk in the natural, so you must learn the ways of the logos, the written Word of God, before you can learn to safely work with *rhema*, the revealed "now" word of God. A solid and balanced working knowledge of the New Testament is the very minimum requirement before you begin to investigate *rhema* revelation in depth. Otherwise, you have no plumbline of measurement.

The Safety of the Family

God has also ordained that we find safety in our relationship to a Bible-believing fellowship. Paul wrote to the Ephesians, "Submit yourselves to one another..." and described many of the areas of covering that God has placed in our lives (see Eph. 5:21 KJV). The Bible says, "In the multitude of counsellors there is safety" (Prov. 11:14b KJV). In an age of lawlessness, we find safety under the umbrella-like covering of the Lord, of His Word, and of the local church. We aren't called to be proud religious rebels "doing our own thing." God has called us to be humble servants committed to a local expression of Christ's Body, diligently studying the Scriptures, praying daily, and being led by the Spirit of Truth into His purposes and individual will for our lives. With this in mind, ask yourself these basic questions before you ever begin your quest to discern God's voice in the spirit realm:

1. Am I regularly studying the Scriptures?

2. Am I maintaining a life of prayer?

3. Am I seeking purity, cleansing, and holiness in my life?

4. Am I a functional member of a local Christian congregation?

These building blocks must be firmly in place before you begin to investigate the principles of testing spiritual experiences. Next I want to urge you to "...examine everything carefully; hold fast to that which is good" (1 Thess. 5:21).

Sources of Revelation

The Scriptures teach us that spiritual revelation or communication comes from any one of three sources: the Holy Spirit, the human soul, and the realm of evil spirits. The need for discernment in this area is obvious.

The Holy Spirit is the only true source of revelation (see 2 Pet. 1:21). It was the Holy Spirit who "moved" the prophets of the Old Testament and the witnesses of the New Testament. The Greek word for "moved," *phero*, means "to be borne along" or even "to be driven along as a wind."[1]

The human soul is capable of voicing thoughts, ideas, and inspirations out of our unsanctifed portion of our emotions (see Ezek. 13:1-6; Jer. 23:16). These human inspirations are not born from God. As Ezekiel the prophet said, they are prophecies "...out of their own hearts...Woe unto the foolish prophets, that follow their own spirit, and have seen nothing" (Ezek. 13:2-3 KJV).

Evil spirits operate with two characteristics common to their master. They can appear as "angels of light" (or as "good voices"), and they always speak lies because they serve the chief liar and the father of lies, satan. Messages delivered through evil spirits are often especially dangerous to people ignorant of God's Word or inexperienced in discernment because satan loves to mix just enough "truth" or factual statements in with his lies to trick gullible people. Just think of it as tasty bait carefully placed in the middle of a deadly trap. Acts 16:16-18 tells about a slave girl with a spirit of divination who *spoke the truth* about the disciples, but got it from a satanic source. When the apostle Paul eventually had heard enough and was irritated within (something just didn't seem right!), he commanded the spirit of divination to leave her.

Dealing With Imperfect People and Mixed Revelation

In a world of imperfect people, God-given revelation can be mixed with competing information from sources that are *not* of God. People functioning as prophetic mouthpieces are imperfect instruments, though vital to the Church today. On the one hand, God warns us, "Do not despise prophetic utterances" (1 Thess. 5:20); but on the other hand, we know that *no prophetic ministry* among human beings is perfect (except that of Christ). All of us must deal with our personal tastes, opinions, and hang-ups when ministering in Christ's name. Peter is one of the most colorful examples of this "mixture" problem in the New Testament. One moment he is speaking strong, current, revelatory words about Jesus' Deity; then minutes later he tries to convince Jesus not to go to the cross! Jesus accurately separated the sources of the two messages and rebuked satan (not Peter) for addressing Him with demonic counsel *through Peter's lips* (see Mt. 16:16-23).

None of us are immune to the effects of outward influences on our lives. Even though God's Spirit is in union with your spirit, you (and I) can be strongly affected in our spirits and souls by such things as the circumstances of life; our physical or bodily circumstances; by satan or his agents; and very often by the other people around us (1 Sam. 1:1-15; 30:12; Jn. 13:2; 1 Cor. 15:33). The solution is to "test" every source and aspect of the revelation. First we test ourselves with a series of self-diagnostic questions.

The "Self" Test

1. Is there any evidence of influences other than the Spirit of God?

2. What is the essence of the "word" or revelation? (How does it compare to God's written Word?)

3. Was I under the control of the Holy Spirit when I received the revelation?

   a. Have I presented my life to Jesus Christ as a living sacrifice?

   b. Have I been obedient to His Word?

   c. Am I being enlightened with His inspiration?

   d. Am I committed to doing His will?

   e. Am I yielding my life to the praises of God or to critical speech?

   f. Am I waiting quietly and expectantly before Him?

The Source Test

The next step is to test whether the image, prophetic message, or vision you received is from your own soulish arena, from satan's realm, or from God. Dr. Mark and Patti Virkler, founders of the Christian Leadership University in Buffalo, New York, offer some excellent guidelines in this area in their landmark work, *Communion With God.* They teach that "the eyes of your heart can be filled by self or satan or God."[2] I've adapted the following guidelines from a table in the Virklers' study guide.[3] The table is preceded by three general instructions:

1. I am to instantly cut off all pictures put before my mind's eye by satan (Mt. 5:28; 2 Cor. 10:5).

2. I am to present the eyes of my heart to the Lord for Him to fill. In this way, I prepare myself to receive (see Rev. 4:1).

3. The Spirit is to project on my inner screen the flow of vision which He desires (see Rev. 4:2).

Testing Whether an Image Is From Self, Satan, or God

A. Find its origin (test the spirit; 1 Jn. 4:1).

   1. *SELF*: Was it primarily born in the *mind*? What does it resemble? How does it feed your ego?

2. *SATAN*: Does the image seem obstructive? Does it lure me away? Is it a flashing image?

3. *GOD*: Is it a "living flow of pictures" coming from my innermost being? Was my inner being quietly focused on Jesus?

B. Examine its content (test the ideas; 1 Jn. 4:5).

1. *SELF*: Does it have ego appeal? Is self the centerpiece or is Jesus the one lifted up?

2. *SATAN*: Is it negative, destructive, pushy, fearful, accusative? Is it a violation of the nature of God? Does it violate the Word of God? Is the image "afraid to be tested"?

3. *GOD*: Is it instructive, uplifting, and comforting? Does it accept testing? Does it encourage you to continue in your walk with God?

C. Seeing its fruit (test the fruit; Mt. 7:16).

1. *SELF*: The fruits here are variable, but eventually they elevate the place of man in contrast to the centrality of Christ.

2. *SATAN*: Are you fearful, compulsive, in bondage, anxious, confused, or possess an inflated ego as a result of the encounter?

3. *GOD*: Do you sense quickened faith, power, peace, good fruit, enlightenment, knowledge, or humility?

Nine Scriptural Tests

Here is a list of nine scriptural tests by which we can test every revelation that we receive for accuracy, authority, and validity.

1. *Does it edify, exhort, or console?* "But one who prophesies speaks to men for *edification* and *exhortation* and *consolation*" (1 Cor. 14:3). The end purpose of all true prophetic revelation is to build up, to admonish, and to

encourage the people of God. Anything that is not directed to this end is not true prophecy. Jeremiah the prophet had to fulfill a negative commission, but even his difficult message contained a powerful and positive promise of God for those who were obedient (see Jer. 1:5,10). First Corinthians 14:26c sums it up best: "Let all things be done unto edification."

2. *Is it in agreement with God's Word?* "All scripture is given by inspiration of God" (2 Tim. 3:16a KJV). True revelation always agrees with the letter and the spirit of Scripture (see 2 Cor. 1:17-20). Where the Holy Spirit says "yea and amen" in Scripture, He also says yea and amen in revelation. He never, ever, contradicts Himself.

3. *Does it exalt Jesus Christ?* "He shall glorify Me; for He shall take of Mine, and shall disclose it to you" (Jn. 16:14). All true revelation centers on Jesus Christ, and exalts and glorifies Him (see Rev. 19:10).

4. *Does it have good fruit?* "Beware of false prophets, who come to you in sheep's clothing, but inwardly are ravenous wolves. You will know them by their fruits..." (Mt. 7:15-16). True revelation produces fruit in character and conduct that agrees with the fruit of the Holy Spirit (see Eph. 5:9; Gal. 5:22-23). Some of the aspects of character or conduct that clearly are not the fruit of the Holy Spirit include pride, arrogance, boastfulness, exaggeration, dishonesty, covetousness, financial irresponsibility, licentiousness, immorality, addictive appetites, broken marriage vows, and broken homes. Any revelation that is responsible for these kinds of results is from a source other than the Holy Spirit.

5. *If it predicts a future event, does it come to pass?* (see Deut. 18:20-22) Any revelation that contains a prediction concerning the future should come to pass. If it doesn't,

then, with a few exceptions, the revelation is not from God. Exceptions may include the following issues:

a. Will of person involved.

b. National repentance—Ninevah repented, so the word did not occur.

c. Messianic predictions. (They took hundreds of years to fulfill).

d. There is a different standard for New Testament prophets than for Old Testament prophets whose predictions played into God's Messianic plan of deliverance.

6. *Does the prophetic prediction turn people toward God or away from Him?* (see Deut. 13:1-5) The fact that a person makes a prediction concerning the future that is *fulfilled* does not necessarily prove that person is moving by Holy Spirit-inspired revelation. If such a person, by his own ministry, turns others away from obedience to the one true God, then that person's ministry is false—even if he makes correct predictions concerning the future.

7. *Does it produce liberty or bondage?* "For you have not received a spirit of slavery leading to fear again, but you have received a spirit of adoption as sons by which we cry out, 'Abba! Father!' " (Rom. 8:15) True revelation given by the Holy Spirit produces liberty, not bondage (see 1 Cor. 14:33; 2 Tim. 1:7). The Holy Spirit never causes God's children to act like slaves, nor does He ever motivate us by fear or legalistic compulsion.

8. *Does it produce life or death?* "Who also made us adequate as servants of a new covenant, not of the letter, but of the Spirit; for the letter kills, but the Spirit gives life" (2 Cor. 3:6). True revelation from the Holy Spirit always produces life, not death.

9. *Does the Holy Spirit bear witness that it is true?* "And as for you, the anointing which you received from Him abides in you, and you have no need for anyone to teach you; but as His anointing teaches you about all things, and is true and is not a lie, and just as it has taught you, you abide in Him" (1 Jn. 2:27). True revelation from the Holy Spirit is always confirmed by the Holy Spirit within the believer. The Holy Spirit is "the Spirit of Truth" (see Jn. 16:13). He *bears witness* to that which is true, but He rejects that which is false. This ninth test is the *most subjective* test of all the tests we've presented here. For that reason, it must be used in conjunction with the previous eight objective standards.

The Spirit Test

The apostle John warns believers of every age:

*Beloved, do not believe every spirit, but **test the spirits to see whether they are from God**; because many false prophets have gone out into the world. By this you know the Spirit of God: every spirit that confesses that Jesus Christ has come in the flesh is from God; and every spirit that does not confess Jesus is not from God; and this is the spirit of the antichrist, of which you have heard that it is coming, and now it is already in the world* (1 John 4:1-3).

As we noted earlier, we have to test the spirits because prophecy, like the other gifts of the Spirit, is delivered through imperfect people. God has chosen to deliver prophecy to the Church through the flawed vessel of humanity. Although "inscripturated revelation" was perfect and inerrant, "prophetic revelation" in the Church of Jesus Christ does not function on this level of inspiration. This is because prophecy isn't our only source or way to hear God's voice. We have the living God dwelling in our hearts and the Holy Spirit leading and guiding each of us each day. Perhaps most importantly, since Calvary, prophecy has served a supportive and secondary role to the Bible, which is God's "more sure Word of prophecy" (see 2 Pet. 1:19), and to the indwelling Spirit of Christ in our hearts.

Another reason discernment is needed is because God has chosen to speak through many people prophetically instead of using just one or two "perfected" people in a generation. Thus there is always the possibility of mixture in the revelatory word, because He chooses to use wounded people with clay feet (see 1 Cor. 14:29). At the same time, every believer has the basic tools to discern truth from falsehood for him or herself. The fact that prophecy is open for judgment in this age proves its present, imperfect state. But remember, the imperfect state of prophecy is directly linked to the imperfect state of the people who deliver it.

The Gift of Discerning of Spirits

Many times the human eye does not immediately discern the true identity of a "wolf" because the outward appearance of the wolf is disguised under "sheep's clothing." However, there is one animal normally connected with the protection of sheep that cannot be deceived by a "sheep's clothing" disguise. That animal is the sheep dog. He is not deceived because he does not judge by his eyesight, but by his sense of smell. *The wolf may look like a sheep, but he still smells like a wolf.*

In Scripture this sense of smell, which acts independently of the sense of sight, may be likened to the spiritual discernment that comes through the Holy Spirit. In Isaiah 11:2-3, the prophet spoke of the ministry of Jesus as the Messiah (the Anointed One), saying that the Spirit of the Lord "...shall make Him of quick understanding [literally, quick of scent] in the fear of the Lord: and He shall not judge after the sight of His eyes, neither reprove after the hearing of His ears" (Is. 11:3 KJV).

Those who care for God's sheep must also be "quick of scent" through the Holy Spirit. They must not judge solely by what they see or correct solely on the basis of what they hear. In this way, they will not depend merely on the evidence of their physical senses or on the reasoning of their natural mind. Shepherds who lean on God's

Spirit will quickly detect the false prophets who come among God's people as "wolves in sheep's clothing."

Any sheep dog that failed to bark when a wolf approached his flock was thought to have failed in his responsibility to the flock. In Isaiah 56:10b (KJV), God condemns Israel's watchmen under the old covenant, saying, "They are all dumb dogs, they cannot bark; sleeping, lying down, loving to slumber." These watchmen failed God and their people. When Israel's spiritual and physical enemies approached, these men remained silent and gave no warning to the flock. As a result, God's people became an easy prey for their enemies. The same thing has happened many times to God's people since then—even in this generation.

All Revelation Is Received by Grace

Any fresh revelation that we receive from God today is a manifestation of God's riches at Christ's expense. It is proof of God's mercy granted to the undeserving and the ill-deserving. It is another evidence that we have received the unmerited favor of God. In many cases, revelation comes through God's *charis*, or grace gifts, listed in First Corinthians chapter 12, as a *charisma*, or "grace made manifest." The Hebrew word for grace, *chen*, means beauty or attractiveness.[4] Its root word, *chanan*, means "favor of a superior toward an inferior."[5]

The word *grace* is used 150 times in the New Testament alone, and mostly in the Epistles. God has dressed His Bride, the Church, with jewels of grace (*charis*), as visible expressions of her Groom's adornment to beautify her. These "gracelets" are the manifested presence of the Holy Spirit in the form of spiritual gifts. By remembering and understanding that any revelation you receive or give to others comes by *grace* alone, you can avoid the pitfall of pride and remain thankful to God at all times. If you don't have the grace of God, you may have the truth, but you won't attract anyone to it. A legalistic "gospel" is unattractive! An understanding of grace, though, helps the vessel through which God's supernatural dimensions come to remain humble and unimpressed with him or herself. Thank the Lord for grace!

Things to Watch for (Whether Receiving or Giving)

Most erroneous revelation is not given to God's people by evil and deceived false prophets. The vast majority of it comes from sincere people who are simply adding their own "hamburger helper" to what starts out as authentic, God-given revelation. They "add" to the nugget of God's prophetic message by drawing from things in their own human psyche, heart, emotions, concern, or sympathy. We need to learn to discern when God has stopped talking and man has continued on. If you are sharing a revelation that God has given you for someone else, be careful to give what God gives and then clearly label or preface anything else you say as your own interpretations and views concerning them.

A second area of common error concerns "revelation" about *things that are already expected or inevitable.* This gets into the "domestic areas" of life, where people try to tell others that they are going to have a baby, the sex of their babies (they have a 50/50 chance of accuracy), and whether or not they will marry. Most married people can have children if they want to, and if they are not married, they will be put under undue pressure, no matter what you say, about their future marital status. Leave these revelations alone or for those with more mature, developed giftings and for special situations.

I urge you to hear the voice or revealed word of God for yourself! Encourage others to do the same. Prophecy, visions, and other forms of revelation can *never* take the place of each individual's hearing God for him or herself. I urge you to cultivate *your own* relationship with Him. Lean your head on your Beloved, and listen to the heart of God for yourself. Lean on your Beloved!

Also remember this: Keep yourself clean and untainted by the habit and spirit of criticism. A critical spirit can infect both your mind and heart, and it can taint what you hear and retain from others. God wants us to be cleansed from all evil reports. He wants our minds and our hearts to be pure before Him so His revelation will not become stained through the filter of criticism or any other unworthy thing.

Final Words of Wisdom

When a fresh breath of the Holy Spirit blows across the Church, as it is at this writing, new and unusual manifestations seem to come with it. Across the world, people are asking, "Are all these manifestations from God? Are all these experiences biblical? Do these encounters bear fruit that remains? Have people 'gone off the deep end' and, in the name of freedom and liberty, cast off the daily spiritual disciplines? Are these manifestations from God or are they a human response to God?"

These are valid questions, and God's Word tells us that we must prove all things and hold fast to that which is good (see 1 Thess. 5:21). In the midst of new and unusual phenomena, we must seek the Lord's wisdom while refusing to use "wisdom" as an excuse for fear. We must be careful not to become offended at the genuine things that the Holy Spirit is doing, no matter how strange they may appear to us. I've listed here 15 "wisdom issues" that cover some of the most common questions and areas of concern that have come up over the years. They will help you to wisely judge the various forms of revelation you will encounter in your adventure with Christ.

15 Wisdom Issues

1. *Search for proper exegesis and scriptural context.* One of the most important issues concerning wisdom is our interpretation of Scriptures— or proper exegesis. Many times, "prophetically gifted" people seem to predominantly take a type of loose symbolic interpretation of Scriptures. Although there are different schools and methodologies of interpretation, we should look for the historical context from which the Scripture is speaking. Wisdom suggests that individuals with revelatory gifts should consult teachers and pastors for greater clarity on scriptural interpretation. Study to show yourself approved (see 2 Tim. 2:15 KJV).

2. *Focus on Jesus.* Manifestations of/to the Holy Spirit should not take center stage—*Jesus* is our central focus.

While giving ourselves to the purposes of God, the movements of the Holy Spirit, and any revelatory word from Heaven, let's not jump on just "any ol' bandwagon." Avoid fads. Sometimes people will jump into anything that's moving because of a lack of security and proper biblical foundation. Remember the simple test: "Does this experience lead me closer to Jesus Christ?"

3. *Major on the "main and plain" things.* Manifestations are not our primary message. In the mainstream of evangelical orthodoxy, our emphasis is to be on the "main and plain" things of Scripture: salvation, justification by faith, sanctification, etc.; followed by the consequential experiences revealed in people's testimonies of how they are advancing in their relationship with God and the community of believers.

4. *Follow biblical principles—not the rigid letter of the Law.* Some things fall into a "non-biblical" category. This does not mean that they are wrong, "of the devil," or contrary to the Scriptures. It just means that there is no sure "biblical text proof" to validate the phenomena. (There was no "proof text" to justify Jesus' spitting in the dirt and anointing a man's eyes with mud either—but it was obviously "right.") Don't stretch something to try to make it fit. Just realize that you might not find a Scripture for every manifestation. So make sure that you are following the clear *principles* of the Word of God.

5. *Build bridges.* In supernatural "times of refreshing," keep in focus the reality that there are other sincere believers who are not as excited about it as you are. This is normal and to be expected. Some of the disciples, such as Thomas, were less excited about the resurrection than others, but they all stood for Christ in the end. Keep yourself clean from spiritual pride and arrogance, and devote yourself to building bridges to the "more cautious" brethren through love, forgiveness, understanding, and kindness.

6. *Honor and pray for leaders.* Realize that every leadership team of a local congregation has the privilege and responsibility to set the tone or the expression of the release of the Spirit in their congregational gatherings. God works through delegated authority! Pray for those in authority with a heart and attitude clean before God. Ask that they be given God's timing, wisdom, and proper game plan. (Be careful and hesitant to apply the label of "controling spirit" or similar titles to leaders! Most leaders are sincere believers who simply want to do what's best for the overall good of their particular flock—and remember, they are God's appointed and anointed.)

7. *Be aware of times and seasons.* Is everything and anything supposed to happen all the time? Apart from a sovereign move of God, I think not. Ecclesiastics 3:1 (KJV) tells us, "To every thing there is a season, and a time for every purpose under the heaven." The Scriptures vividly depict "Pentecost meetings," but you will also find clear admonitions from Paul on how to walk with those in the "room of the ungifted or unbeliever" as well. We should never use our freedom to offend others. I personally believe that it is in line with God's Word to have specific meetings for predetermined specific purposes. The leading of the Spirit works both ways. You can predetermine by His guidance that certain nights or meetings are "refreshing gatherings" as well as "fall into" those spontaneous occurrences when His manifest Presence is released.

8. *Let love rule.* The "unusual and rare" is not to be our consistent diet, nor will it ever replace the daily Christian spiritual disciplines. If all a person does is "bark like a dog" and quits reading the Scriptures and relating properly to other members of the local church, then most likely some other spirit is at work. Perhaps the individual has simply lost focus and needs a word spoken in love to help him or her maintain spiritual equilibrium in the

midst of a mighty outpouring. Whatever the case, let love always be the rule.

9. *Maintain balance.* There is no exact science for figuring out all the manifestations of/to the Holy Spirit. When something is unclear, don't over-define what you don't understand. There is a godly tightrope of dynamic tension between the reality of subjective experience and biblical doctrine. Let us strive to maintain our balance!

10. *Understand the relationship of divine initiation and human response.* Is all this laughter (or crying, shaking, falling, and making noise, etc.) from God? I specifically call these "manifestations of/to the Holy Spirit" for a very good reason. Although some of these external, visible, and audible signs are divinely initiated, we must admit that some of them are human responses and reactions to the Holy Spirit's movement upon us or upon others close by. Divine initiative is followed by human response. This is normal.

11. *Be known by your fruits.* Although we want to bless what we see the Father doing, let's also direct this blessing into fruitful works. If we have been truly refreshed, then we must channel it into *practical works* that express our faith. Let's channel this energy from a "bless me club" into a "bless others" focus that feeds the hungry and ministers to the poor, the widow, the orphan, and the single parent. Channel God's life into evangelism, intercession, worship, and other things that display the passion and compassion of Jesus for people.

12. *Perceive the works of God and the motives of man.* Although the phenomena of shaking, laughing, weeping, shouting, falling, and other bizarre manifestations have occurred in revivals throughout Church history, I doubt that you can make a case for any of these individuals *trying* to do these things. These experiences were equated

with receiving an anointing for power in ministry and as tools of radical means whereby God brought personal transformation.

13. *Control your flesh and cooperate with God.* Do you remember the fruit of the Spirit of self-control (see Gal. 5:23)? Too many of us have forgotten it or thrown it out the window! Nowhere in the Scriptures are we told that we are to "control God"—we are told to control "self." The fruit of self-control is to conquer the deeds of the flesh—lust, immorality, party spirit, etc. We are to cooperate with and yield to the Presence of God and control the deeds of the flesh.

14. *Be alert and aware.* Let us search Scripture, review Church history, seek the Lord, and receive input from those who are wiser and more experienced than we. Seasoned believers know that the enemy always tries to "club" Christians over the head after they've had a renewal and fresh experience, in hopes that they will become confused, discouraged, and bewildered. Arm yourself. This is a real war. This refreshment isn't just "fun and games." It is to lead us into greater effectiveness for our Master!

15. *Avoid spiritual ditches.* There are two deep ditches you should avoid. Watch out for *analytical skepticism.* It causes you to be offended by what you don't understand. The other deadly ditch is *fear* (of man, rejection, fanaticism, etc.). Both of these "ditches" have a common fruit: criticism. Consider this nugget of wisdom:

If you can't jump in the middle of it, bless it.
If you can't bless it, then patiently observe it.
If you can't patiently observe it, just don't criticize it!

Fearing God, Not the Devil

I'm sorry to say that some churches have taught people to be afraid of the devil instead of emphasizing the completed work of the cross and the authority of the believer. Although we need to have a healthy respect for the powers of darkness, we are never taught in the Scriptures to fear the devil. Let's turn on the light of truth and expose the deception of the evil one.

We are taught in Scripture to "fear God and keep His commandments" (Eccles. 12:13). Let's trust our Father, ask for the gift of the Holy Spirit in Jesus' name, and expect for true, authentic supernatural encounters of the heavenly kind to come down. Let's fear God, not the devil, and believe that our Father will give us good gifts.

Pray this prayer with me right where you are, and allow the Spirit of the Lord to seal these things in your spirit and life through prayer:

> *Your Word tells us to not despise prophesying, to test all things, and to hold fast to what is good. We lift up Your Word as our standard. Help us to be wise stewards of Your grace, dear Lord. Teach us to discern good from evil. Grant us the fear of the Lord and the wisdom applications of properly judging revelation. In Jesus' mighty name, amen.*

Endnotes

1. James Strong, *Strong's Exhaustive Concordance of the Bible* (Peabody, Massachusetts: Hendrickson Publishers, n.d.), **moved** (Greek, #5342).

2. Mark and Patti Virkler, *Communion With God* (Shippensburg, Pennsylvania: Destiny Image Publishers, 1990), 77.

3. Virkler, *Communion With God*, adapted from a diagram (78) and from a table entitled "Testing Whether an Image Is From Self, Satan or God" (79). Used by permission.

4. *Strong's Exhaustive Concordance*, **grace** (Hebrew, #2580).

5. *Strong's Exhaustive Concordance*, **favor**, (Hebrew, #2603).

Chapter 11

Keys to the Supernatural

Jim W. Goll

The Spirit of the Lord [is] upon Me, because He has anointed Me [the Anointed One, the Messiah] to preach the good news (the Gospel) to the poor; He has sent Me to announce release to the captives and recovery of sight to the blind, to send forth as delivered those who are oppressed [who are downtrodden, bruised, crushed, and broken down by calamity], to proclaim the accepted and acceptable year of the Lord [the day when salvation and the free favors of God profusely abound] (Luke 4:18-19 AMP).

What are some of the keys that will help unlock the supernatural? God's Word tells us that a "threefold cord is not quickly broken" (see Eccles. 4:12 KJV). This principle shows up throughout the Bible and God's dealings with us. It should be no surprise that there are three interwoven cords or keys that God gives us to unlock His supernatural wonders and riches in this life. They are faith, His manifested presence, and "imparters," or anointed and gifted people, whom He places in our lives.

Various Dimensions of Faith

Faith is at the root of every blessing and work of God. But many of us have a deceptively simple idea about faith that sometimes limits us to thoughts of, *Well, my faith isn't very great, so it will never happen to me.* The truth is that there are several categories of faith.

The first category comes at "birth." The moment we are born again in Christ, God *gives* each of us what the Bible calls "a measure of faith." This free allotment of faith must be *exercised* before it can increase (see Rom. 12:3-8). A person's muscles grow because they are used, pushed, and exercised. It is the same with believers—exercise the faith you have and things will take shape! But we each have faith—a measure of faith.

The second category of faith comes through *development.* Every believer who yields to the continuous work of the Holy Spirit in their lives will *bear spiritual fruit.* It is inevitable and even mandatory. One of the fruits of the Holy Spirit that should rise up in your life is called "faithfulness" (see Gal. 5:22-23). It deals with the character of God being revealed in your life— things like being trustworthy. The Holy Spirit will develop honest, enduring fruit in our lives called faithfulness.

This third category comes purely as a *gift*, so Paul called it the "gift of faith" in First Corinthians 12:9. It is a special surge of confidence in God and His Word as it rises up in someone faced with a specific situation or need (see Mk. 11:22-24). It can come to *anyone* who belongs to Christ and is distributed as the Holy Spirit sees fit (see 1 Cor. 12:7).

Faith is a necessity for all of us. It is a marvelous key that unlocks the supernatural in our lives. Faith comes (present active tense) and continues to come by the words (*rhema*) of Christ (see Rom. 10:17). Let us be people of faith in a supernatural God. But remember, faith is always spelled one way: R-I-S-K. We must step out of our comfort zones to exercise our measure of faith.

The gift of faith can be expressed through *words of faith spoken to God* on behalf of a person, an object, or a situation. An Old

Testament example is seen in the ministry of Elijah the prophet who spoke to God and commanded the rain, the dew, and the end of drought by faith (see 1 Kings 17:1; 18:41-45; compare Jas. 5:16-18). Many times this happens when we receive the gift of faith to pray for the sick or an apparently impossible situation. This gift can also be exercised in *words spoken directly to a person*, an object, or a situation on behalf of God. Joshua, for instance, spoke to the sun and moon on behalf of God (see Josh. 10:12-14). In this instance, we would not only pray for the sick, but we also would speak by supernatural faith, "Be healed in the name of Jesus." (Caution, consideration, and wisdom are obviously needed in these situations.)

God's Tangible Presence

The second great cord in this rope of supernatural encounters is the manifested (or openly revealed and tangible) Presence of God among us. There are times when the power of the Holy Spirit is especially tangible to perform signs and wonders among us. Luke 5:17 says, "...and the power of the Lord was present for Him [Jesus] to perform healing." Another time, Jesus was walking in the anointing of God in the middle of a crowd, but only the "woman with the issue of blood" had the faith to "plug into" the manifested Presence of God and receive her healing (see Mk. 5:21-34, especially verse 30).

At other times, God seems to impart a "lingering" or resident measure of His Presence upon geographical regions where He has done great things in the past or even upon objects to set them apart for His own purposes. The Bible tells us that when some mourners threw the body of a man into Elisha's grave (because they had sighted some raiders heading their way), they were shocked when the dead man suddenly stood up alive after his body came into contact with Elisha's bones (see 2 Kings 13:21). There are also what I call Holy Spirit "power points" in geographical regions where God has released astounding supernatural power for His divine purpose. The evangelist, Duncan Campbell, described what appeared to be a "radiation zone" of God's power that appeared during the Hebrides Islands revival. Everyone who came near it— sinner or saint— was strongly affected by God's manifest Presence. These experiences could be called "opened heavens," "portals of His Presence," etc. Whatever term you use to describe this phenomena, we need the release of God's tangible Presence.

There is an issue of faith that must be settled for each one of us. You have heard ministers say, "Oh, the anointing is strong here." That is great! But we must learn to, through faith, tap into the strength of anointing that lives inside of us as born-again believers. Christ, the Anointed One, lives in us. We must learn to draw forth from the well of salvation of the anointing of His Presence within us, and bring it (actually Him) forth and give cups of His Presence to those around us.

Imparters: Releasing the Power of His Presence

The apostle Paul wrote to the believers in Rome, "For I long to see you in order *that I may impart* some spiritual gift to you, that you may be established" (Rom. 1:11). Paul was an "imparter," a gifted servant of God who was used by God to share, impart, or pass along the things that God had given him. He told his young disciple, Timothy, "...I remind you to kindle afresh the gift of God which is in you through the laying on of my hands" (2 Tim. 1:6). Earlier in his life, Paul (then known as Saul) was the recipient of things imparted to him by Ananias (see Acts 9:17).

In the Old Testament, God used Moses to impart the anointing to lead Israel to Joshua (see Deut. 34:9); and Elijah to impart a double mantle of anointing to Elisha (see 1 Kings 19:15-21; 2 Kings 2:1-12). Even the wayward King Saul was transformed into "another man" when he came under the influence of the prophetic presence and influence of God upon others (see 1 Sam. 10:5-12; 19:20-24). God is using imparters today as well. They are used to bring "jumper cables" onto the weakened batteries of our lives and charge us up. Michal Ann and I have benefited tremendously from the experience, blessing, and gifting of others. We are indebted to God for the impartations He has brought us through the anointing upon Mahesh Chavda, the spirit of prayer upon Dick Simmons, the prophetic grace upon Bob Jones, and the fire of God upon Jill Austin. We are grateful for these and so many others. May the Lord bring imparters into your lives as well. Catch the Presence of Christ and give it away!

Additional Keys:
Compassion, God's Revealed Will, and Divine Timing

You must have compassion if you want to move in the powerful and supernatural Presence of God. As we noted in Chapter 5, this compassion is imparted to us by our heavenly Father who always demonstrates His compassion to us. We are to have the same compassion Jesus had, which according to author Ken Blue, was "...not merely an expression of His will but rather an eruption from deep within His being. Out of this compassion of Jesus sprang His mighty works of rescue, healing, and deliverance."1 The Holy Spirit wants us to have God's heart on a matter and to release an expression of compassion through us. Have you been stirred within and find yourself bursting to see God break through?

The will and the Word of God are paramount in all demonstrations of Holy Spirit ministry. Although you may grow tired of hearing this, it must be repeated again: No matter what activity of the Spirit you see or are involved in, it must match up and conform to the revealed will of God outlined in His Word, the Bible (see 1 Jn. 3:21-24; 5:15). What does God's Word say? What is His revealed will? You must apprehend this knowledge to be able to move out in the anointing with confidence.

What time is it? Has the strategic timing of God come for the release of this activity? Supernatural signs often are released by God at just the appointed moment—and not until. You see, there are two different words in the Greek New Testament language for the word *time*. They are the words *chronis* and *kairos*. *Chronis* is used to refer to a sequential order of time—a chronology. *Kairos*, on the other hand, refers to a specific strategic moment. What time is it? Has the *kairos* appointment of God's calendar appeared?

You also need to be sensitive to the Spirit of God. It is no accident that the Word of God says, "And the spirits of the prophets are subject to the prophets" (1 Cor. 14:32 KJV). For one thing, that means we don't have to "blurt out" the things that God reveals the very moment He speaks to us. He is not the author of confusion, so He knows exactly when and how your particular "piece of the supernatural puzzle" is to fit into place, and He will work within the authority structure that He has established (see 1 Cor. 14:33). Always ask yourself, "When does God want this supernatural act demonstrated, and why?"

Releasing the Supernatural

You have prepared yourself to receive supernatural revelation from God, and once it came, you examined yourself, your source, and the content of your message. You have been careful to fit into the plan, purpose, order, and timing of God—now how do you *release* the supernatural? Part of the answer is found in the ministries of those who have gone before us.

Chapter 16 in the Book of First Samuel describes the day that Samuel the prophet was sent to anoint the son of Jesse in backwater Bethlehem. The problem was that Jesse had a *lot* of sons. Samuel was all filled up with anointing and his ram's horn was full of anointing oil—the problem was he didn't know exactly upon whom to release it. He couldn't trust his natural instincts—God warned him about that (see 1 Sam. 16:7). Even though he didn't know everything, he knew enough to get him going. Often we don't get more information till we have stepped out in faith with the little bit we already possess.

Samuel Prayed Through Every Option

Samuel begins and assumes that the firstborn son would be the one to receive the anointing. After all, the firstborn had the birthright. He proceeds to begin anointing him, but the Holy Spirit stops him. I have found through years of ministry that we need to do what Samuel did in this situation. He prayed through all seven sons (now it would really be hard for some of us to pass up the firstborn and then the seventh one also—after all, doesn't God know His own rules?) But still the Spirit did not say, "this is the one!" Finally Jesse pulled David—the forgotten eighth son—out of the fields and at last God allowed Samuel to release

His supernatural anointing. Remember, we tend to look on the outward, but God looks on the heart. It is especially important for us in times of strategic decision-making or ministry situations to *pray through* all the choices or directions present. Let each one pass "under the rod" of God's discernment and anointing! Have faith in God. He will confirm to you the one(s) whom He chooses!

Simeon Kept Looking Until He Saw God's Anointed

Another model of ministry is found in the patient life of Simeon. We need to have the eyes of Simeon, the aged saint who won a promise from God that he could live until he saw with his own eyes God's anointed Messiah (see Lk. 2:25-35). Simeon fervently sought God until he received a divine promise of supernatural revelation. Then he continued in patient "waiting and watching" until his promise came to pass. At that point Simeon confirmed with divine authority in the Spirit what had taken place and painted a prophetic picture of what was to come.

We, like Jesus, are to do those things that we see the Father doing (see Jn. 5:19). Have you waited on the Lord? Have you been watching to see what He might speak to you? May the Holy Spirit open the eyes of our heart and grant the "seer" grace so that we too can do the works of Christ.

Pioneering and Multiplying in the Spirit

We've already discussed the role of "imparters" in the Church, but we need to realize that God often uses these "imparters" as Holy Ghost "fire starters" and point people who pioneer new vistas, outreaches, and growth in the Spirit. Their principle purpose is to get others going, to equip them for their God-ordained tasks, and to turn them loose as well. Our central goal is to see the *multiplication* of God's glorious Presence in the earth.

Our dear brother, Randy Clark, pastor of the St. Louis Vineyard Christian Fellowship, is truly one of God's "fire starters" for this generation. He, and many others, are being used to light the fires of God's Presence in different geographic regions as others come from far and near to "catch the fire" and spread it wherever they go. I also think of cataclysmic ministry of Wes and Stacey Campbell in Kelowna, British Columbia, Canada. Passivity has no future around these bravehearts. Lord, light the fire again! Raise up Your tried champions who carry the torch for their generation and impart it to others.

The Importance of Waiting and Worship

You can generally measure the value that people put toward something by the amount of patience they exhibit when trying to acquire it. Although people are usually unwilling to stay very long in a church service, they will gladly spend the night on the street to get tickets to the Super Bowl or the World Series! God knows our frame (see Ps. 103:14). He knows that when we practice the godly attribute of patience solely to capture His Presence, then we have placed a great value on the things that are nearest His heart. Patient waiting draws the Spirit's Presence to us.

Waiting is a magnet that woos His coming. The Holy Spirit spoke to a noted prophetic minister and friend named John Paul Jackson, saying, "Tell them, *if they'll wait*, I will come." Worship is tied closely to this. Even a casual reading of the Gospels will reveal that *worship* was the attitude and posture of many who came to Jesus for a supernatural touch. They often bowed down in reverent worship before making and receiving their request. As you wait upon Him and worship Him, let your faith go up to Him and expect great things! He loves to bless those who anticipate and expect great things from Him by faith. Waiting and worship fit together like a hand in a glove.

Wisdom in Handling Revelation

Let's go on to a complementary subject. We have looked at some of the keys to the supernatural, but are there wisdom ways we must learn here also? Divine revelation is like a pot of boiling water on a stove. You need to put on the mittens of wisdom to carry the pot and its contents to a place of usefulness and purpose. Otherwise, it will spill on you! And you can be burned by it if you *mishandle* it.

Every gift and revelation of God is like a loaded weapon or powerful medicine in your hands—if you handle it loosely and unwisely, it can hurt and destroy instead of heal and build up. If you discern a problem in a certain situation and fail to seek God's wisdom on how to administer it, your gift of discernment can become a tool of gossip that burns and destroys the lives of others. Remember Proverbs 12:8: "A man will be praised according to his insight...." Ask for God's "insight with wisdom and understanding."

Tips for Beginners

1. When you've received something from the Lord for someone else, turn it into a question as you present it to him: "Does this mean anything to you?" Be humble in your approach, not a "know-it-all"!

2. Turn your revelation into intercession. Pray the inspiration instead of sweating out heavy perspiration. Pray the promise back to God!

3. Submit your impressions (revelation) to trusted counsel. God will not give it all to you anyway. Trust Him to speak through others as well.

4. Realize that if you've received the genuine article, there is a natural tension that comes with it: *Do I sit on this or run with it?* This tension is a normal part of your learning curve. He will teach you what to do!

5. Learn the lesson quick and well from Proverbs 29:11a (KJV): "A fool uttereth all his mind." Don't be a fool. Ask the Holy Spirit questions and watch and learn from others for answers to these questions as well: "What do I say? To whom do I give it? When do I release it? Where do I present it?" Most of us learn this proverb by experience!

6. As you grow, eventually another situation will come. You will be praised because of your (really His) gift. What will you do with these trophies that people bring to you?

Noted Bible teacher Bob Mumford, years ago, said, "At the end of the day, I present my trophies to the Lord and I worship Him with them."

Words to the Wise

Learn how to wisely respond to "second heaven revelation." Different groups and individuals refer to this in a variety of terms and ways, but not every revelation you receive is a declaration of what is supposed to come to pass. At times the Holy Spirit may give you insight into one of satan's schemes or plans. Don't be alarmed; Paul said we are not to be ignorant of the devil's schemes (see 2 Cor. 2:11). The term, "second heaven revelation," refers to information we receive concerning the enemy's camp or evil plans. God gives us these insights to enlighten and forewarn us so we can either prepare for it beforehand or to cut it off through intercession before it even occurs (God's will and plan determines which one).

Be careful with your curiosity. Is it the Holy Spirit who is leading you into this new experience? Is it your soulish desires or is it divine initiative? Are you being led by your passion for Jesus or is an enticing spirit leading you toward darkness by pulling on your curiosity? Many people have found themselves drawn toward the occult, supposedly for the purpose of "learning the enemy's devices," and end up entangled in deception. The fruit is distinctly different. With an enticing spirit you are left "beat up" and discouraged. When God is your guide on the journey of the supernatural, you are left enlightened and empowered.

Give your revelation with gentleness (see Gal. 6:1; 2 Tim. 2:23-26). The wisest path is to minister in brokenness. Hard confrontation is the exception, not the norm. If your revelation involves rebuke or correction, go through the standard procedures of first speaking, second exhorting, and third warning with all authority according to the biblical pattern in Titus 2:18. Gentleness is the tool that disarms fear and builds the bridge that allows the cargo to cross.

Realize that some words are conditional, and some revelations are given without the condition being spoken. Consider God's word to Jonah about Nineveh being destroyed in 40 days. Was it? No, because the people of Nineveh took God's prophet seriously and repented. Jonah was tried himself by the revelations given him. But eventually God showed him the true purpose of His pronounced judgment— restoration and compassionate redemption (see Jon. 3:4– 4:11). *Behind every word of judgment stands a merciful God ready to forgive.* Again, consider the example found in Amos 7. He was given five visions of judgment, and they were true revelatory experiences. Yet Amos' intercession blocked two of the five prophecies from coming to pass (40 percent)! This again is an example of a merciful God! Make sure that your revelatory ministry is saturated with mercy and grace and not haughty pride.

Wisdom shouts the fear of the Lord (see Prov. 9:10). Never use your revelation as a tool of punishment. The Holy Spirit spoke to me once, "Be careful not to stretch the rod of your mouth out against the House that the Lord builds." Work with God— not against Him and His appointed leaders. Put on the fear of the Lord.

Don't borrow and snatch! Avoid using another person's revelation as your own to gain credibility before man. If necessary, ask the other person if you have permission to restate his or her prophetic word. And give proper credit. When asked by others about another person's word, stand secure and simply say, "I don't know. You will have to consult him."

Avoid being tainted by an evil report. You can become tainted by listening to one person give an evil report about someone else under the *guise* of revelation. We all need to read and learn the truths found in chapters 13 and 14 of the Book of Numbers. Then we need to be cleansed by the blood of Jesus from the defilement of evil reports and gossip. Remember, it's about the gift of discernings of spirits—not gossip concerning another's problems.

Be alert to the activity of the "accuser of the brethren." Satan seeks every opportunity to spew his filthy stew of accusation on believers (see Rev. 12:10). Peter warned us, "...be on the alert. Your adversary, the devil, prowls about like a roaring lion, seeking someone to devour" (1 Pet. 5:8). Fall out of agreement with the devil! Speak, release, and declare the medicine of life into broken situations.

Don't throw away your relationship with God. No matter how high the level of prophetic activity gets around you, don't depend primarily on the "ears" of others. This was the situation of the Old Testament. The Spirit of God dwells in *you*, so you must hear God for yourself! Read chapter 13 of First Kings (especially verse 1) concerning an intense account of prophetic activity. Get your own revelation from God; don't let someone else hear for you. You must hear God for yourself *first* and let others be used to confirm it!

The Five Don'ts of Supernatural Ministry

1. *Never allow the things you hear through others become a substitute for hearing the voice of the Holy Spirit for yourself.* This also means that you should never allow the revelations you hear coming from men override your devotion or total loyalty to the Scriptures (see 1 Kings 13). God is a jealous God (see Ex. 20:5). He wants you to spend time with Him! Keep to the basics!

2. *Never lift up the vessel who brings the word.* Lift up Jesus! Remember, the testimony of Jesus is the spirit of prophecy (see Rev. 19:10). Let Jesus truly be the chief prophet in our midst! Remember God's solemn warning in the Book of Isaiah, "And My glory I will not give to another" (Is. 48:11b). We live in an age of mercy and grace, but God has drawn clear limits where His glory is concerned.

3. *Don't be naive.* "The naive believes everything, but the prudent man considers his steps" (Prov. 14:15). Do not

believe every spirit! Test the spirits to see if they be of God (see 1 Jn. 4:1-6). Ask for wisdom (see Jas. 1:5; Ps. 25:4).

4. *Don't twist the meaning of the revelation or word.* Don't twist the meaning of the word to comply with your desires, wishes, hidden agenda, mixed motives, timing, or aspirations. Hold onto the words with "open 'no-strings-attached' expectancy" that our supernatural God will fulfill His words in whatever manner He chooses. Don't treat prophetic experiences as a taffy pull—pulling and stretching it to fit your desired need.

5. *Do not quench the Holy Spirit.* First of all, don't "despise prophesyings" (see 1 Thess. 5:19-21 KJV). (Some people who have a prophetic ministry mysteriously don't want to receive or acknowledge the prophecies of anyone else!) Counterfeit prophecies and mixture do occur, but don't be disillusioned. Keep in mind that there are two ditches to avoid. One is the despising and disdaining of the supernatural. The other ditch is that of fascination and being enamored. But don't let failure stop you! Believe God for His full restoration of pure prophetic ministry. It is worth the journey.

The Five Do's of Supernatural Ministry

1. *Earnestly desire the gifts of the Holy Spirit.* In the words of the apostle Paul, "...desire...especially that you may prophesy" (1 Cor. 14:1). Not only does God want to speak *to* you, but He also wants to speak *through* you! Desire the gift of prophecy!

2. *Believe God's prophets and you will succeed* (see 2 Chron 20:20). Rejoice! What a privilege you have been given. All you have to do is mix faith with God's words and receive the Lord's results. But always remember to place your faith "in the *God* of the *Word*, not in the *man* of the *word*."

3. *Pray the promise back to God.* Follow Daniel's example of respectfully and humbly reminding God of His word through intercession (see Jer. 29:10; Dan. 9:1-19). Bathe the prophetic invitation in prayer.

4. *Fight the good fight.* Use the spoken *rhema* word of prophecy in your life as equipment for spiritual battle (see 1 Tim. 1:18). Do spiritual warfare against discouragement, doubt, unbelief, and fear through declaring and reciting the prophecies given over your life.

5. *Seek confirmation at all times.* Remember the biblical measure of validity: "Out of the mouth of two or three witnesses every fact is to be confirmed and established" (see Deut. 19:15; Mt. 18:16; 2 Cor. 13:1). Walk with others and seek the mind of Christ through godly counsel.

Develop the Character to Carry the Gift

There are generally two kinds of ministries in the Church: the "shooting star" and the "North star." One rises fast, blazes bright, and draws much attention with a flashy ministry that burns furiously for a short while and then quickly fades in a moral failure or fatal character flaw right in front of everyone. On the other hand, the "North star" ministry is fixed, stable, and consistent. It may not be as flashy, but it has been used to give guidance to many on the seas of uncertainty for generations without wavering or wallowing in sin.

The people with a "shooting star" approach to ministry have chosen to seek a single anointing—they are going for the fullness of God's power without waiting for the fullness of God's character. This does involve waiting because it must be "grown" into us through experience and countless small and great obediences. They pay virtually nothing up front, but they pay dearly in the end.

The believers with a "North star" ministry approach have chosen the best kind. But they "pay the cost" every day by taking up their cross and following Jesus and obeying His commands step by painful step. They have submitted themselves to God's will that they may be "confirmed to His image." As a result, they have earned a *double anointing* of the fullness of God's *character* and the fullness of God's *power* in their lives. This is how you develop "the character to carry the gift."

"Going for the Double"

On Mother's Day in 1994, I decided to give Michal Ann a very special Mother's Day present. The best thing I could think of was to pray for her. As I began to pray, my spiritual eyes were opened for a moment and I saw a clear crystal pitcher over Ann's head. It had the number "9" with a "2" etched above it, and I realized that it signified the mathematical term, "nine to the second power." Then I heard the words in my spirit, "We are going for the double this time."

I watched as this beautiful pitcher was tipped down and clear water poured out upon Michal Ann's head. It seemed to literally go down inside her being. The Holy Spirit said, "I am going to teach you about 'the double.' You have heard that Elisha asked a difficult thing—he asked for a double of the anointing that rested upon Elijah and thus he received. We are going for 'the double' this time." I continued to watch as the water poured into my wife, and it seemed that brown sediment was pushed down deep inside her (as it is with all of us!). Then light brown water began pouring out of her as the clear water kept pouring in from above. The more the water flowed through her, the clearer the water became that proceeded outward. Eventually the water emerging from her being was as clear as the water going in.

Again, I heard the words, "We are going for 'the double' this time—the fullness of character and the fullness of power." Instantly I understood that the "nine to the second power" symbol etched on the pitcher signified the joining of the nine fruits of the Holy Spirit (the fullness of character) with the nine gifts of the Spirit (the fullness of power).

God is going to continue to pour His living waters into each one of us to flush away the hurts, bitterness, and debris that we try to hide. He is determined to make us into vessels that contain His glory. In our pursuit of the keys to the supernatural, let's cooperate with the work of the cross in our lives, in order that we might have the character to carry the gift. Why don't you pray this prayer with me right where you are:

Heavenly Father, Your Son, Jesus, said that "greater works than these" shall we do. Father, I want You to release a demonstration of Your greatness through my life. I want to see the greater works in my generation. Grant to me the keys to the supernatural and give me the character to carry the gift. I ask for this special grace in Jesus' name and for the rewards of Christ's suffering. Amen.

Endnote

1. Ken Blue, *The Authority to Heal* (Downers Grove, Illinois: InterVarsity Press, 1987), 76.

Chapter 12

Pursue the God of Visitation

Michal Ann Goll

Beloved, I implore you as aliens and strangers and exiles [in this world] to abstain from the sensual urges (the evil desires, the passions of the flesh, your lower nature) that wage war against the soul. Conduct yourselves properly (honorably, righteously) among the Gentiles, so that, although they may slander you as evildoers, [yet] they may by witnessing your good deeds [come to] glorify God in the day of inspection [when God shall look upon you wanderers as a pastor or shepherd looks over his flock] (1 Peter 2:11-12 AMP).

This passage applies to many different times of divine visitation to mankind throughout history, although it may be a specific reference to that one great day of the second coming of the Lord Jesus Christ. In these times of divine visitation, the manifested or revealed Presence of God has literally come into our "time/space world" to invade our unholy comfort zones with His glory. In those moments, the limits of passing time and living in our single-dimension world fall to the wayside as the Creator of time, who fills and maintains all things, turns our world upside down. Our old concepts and paradigms are radically shifted as He comes to reveal the eternal aspects of His personality, His character, His power, and His loveliness. Yet more than any of these, God comes in times of divine visitation to *reveal Himself.*

Whether God reveals Himself to individuals or to entire generations in the course of unfolding Church history, those times of awakening and visitation will forever change our lives—if we let them. When God enters the front stage of our lives, our favorite defining statement becomes: "We're not who we were, we're not who we want to be, and we're not yet who we're going to be." We need to learn how to live with one another in the Body of Christ according to the truth in this statement. We should all wear placards around our necks that say in very large, loud letters, "Under Construction. Hard Hats Required. Beware of Falling Sins, Fears, and Large Egos."

One of the very best things that could have happened to Jim and I was the talk we had in our kitchen after God began to change me through the nine weeks of angelic visitations. It opened our eyes, and it helped us to come into agreement on one of the most important issues of life: *Change is inevitable.* Jim knew that he "liked me the way I was" (before the Lord began to visit me in the night). He was watching closely the things that were happening to me. Transition, change, and uncertainty were the rule of the day. But, together, by God's grace, we had confidence that if I became more like God, then he would like me even better! But Jim had to face the hard issues, that the closer I got to the Lord, the greater would be the new levels of conviction. Nevertheless, Jim pressed in and aligned himself with God's work in my life, even though it surprised and even alarmed him at times. Now we are entering into new levels of wisdom, understanding, partnership, and adventure as we step out into new things with God. I have to admit that these are some of the most fun times I have ever had, but I've also had my uncomfortable and frightening moments!

Has God Gone Home Already?

The same thing is happening in the Body of Christ around the world. Many different branches of the Church are discovering that they need certain giftings (gifts invested in people) that have been silent for a long time in the Church. Some of the current church leaders who are strong in their gifts and position are used to being the "chief mouthpiece of God" to their churches. At times, they are so used to talking that they just keep on talking and talking and talking—long after God has gone home. That is because they are used to doing that.

Obviously there is going to be a natural tension in the Body of Christ when God raises up new giftings with a command to speak. The Church is in transition right now, and many of us will have to learn how to give and take under the direction of the Holy Spirit. Many who talk loudly or who are used to listening to loud talkers will have to learn how to listen for the quiet voice of God and to let Him speak in a whisper whenever and however He desires. For some, it's time to be Dumbo—all ears in order to fly. For others, it is time to take the wire trap of intimidation off their mouths, and speak!

There are too many people in the Body of Christ who are out of place and out of joint. Yes, there is a prophetic gifting that is alive and active in their lives, but they are frustrated because the life that God put in them has been constricted in little man-made boxes. Too many times we have placed narrow, rigid man-made definitions on God-made gifts—and the two have *never, ever, mixed*. When these limited definitions are promoted as "God-inspired" job descriptions, then the people whom God has anointed with supernatural gifts will naturally try to function within those politically correct definitions. Why? That's the only way they know how to operate! The truth is that they are operating in a very limited form of the full spiritual gifting that God has for them. The Lord is about to release a wider spectrum of His prophetic spirit on His people, and although I hope we will be slow to slap new "definitions" on them, we do know that God will introduce totally new avenues and ways of expressing the Father's heart to this generation.

Untold thousands of people with revelatory gifts are sitting in our church pews, attending Sunday school classes, and singing in our services, but their heavenly gifts have been mute in our local churches. They've been quiet because they've been squelched by the low expectations or limited understanding of others, as well as by their own fears—but God is getting ready to open the door. He is getting ready to raise up a prophetic song that is destined to pass far beyond the four walls and front doors of our church buildings. This wonderful prophetic presence must invade the marketplace of the world in order for true, authentic change to come about.

Now She's Free!

I saw a glimpse of this in a dream I had in which I started to sing a prophetic song in a large shopping mall. I didn't even care where I was because my heart and mind were consumed with the Light of His life. I was literally dancing around non-Christian people with my purse slung around my shoulder as I sang out the song of the Lord, and I heard the words, "Now she's free."

There is something about the "quietness" of this new prophetic generation that creates a certain awe among non-believers and believers alike. I believe that it is because it would take a miracle to get such quiet and meek people to act so boldly and powerfully. God is ready to release the wealth of dormant giftings in His Church, and we need to be prepared for it. As Jim and I discovered that night in our kitchen, we each have to learn to listen to one another. Jim knew he would have to step back from the spokesman position from time to time in order to make room for the gift that God had raised up in me, and he did so. There are many other strong leaders who won't be so willing or so successful during this transition.

The pressure is on the existing leaders in the Body of Christ to listen and recognize where God's anointing is resting in the days to come. I think the anointing of God is going to come from some places that we would never have expected to see it. This isn't a new phenomenon in a sense. Jesus tapped the anointing in rough

fishermen at the seashore, in despised tax collectors, in religious fa-
natics who advocated the violent overthrow of Rome, and in the
same "religious seminary" setting where His enemies ordered His
crucifixion. (In the latter I'm speaking of the Lord's choice of Saul,
the star pupil of Israel's top-ranking rabbi and Pharisee, Gamaliel.)

None of the Lord's disciples would have been invited to speak
at most of our churches today—they didn't have any degrees,
pedigrees, or social standing. If we want to tap the Peter anointing, the Paul anointing, the John anointing, and the James anointing that are lying dormant in our churches, then it will take
discerning hearts and eyes to see them, and grace-filled leaders to
make room for them.

Look How Far We've Come

When Jim and I met, I was teaching the adult Sunday school
class in the tiny Methodist church I'd attended all my life. My
class of ten adults even included a few men, and I suppose that
was remarkable for the time and setting. I was relatively well
qualified to teach the class. I had read my Bible every day from
the time I learned to read; I prayed every day; and I had a loving
relationship with God.

When Jim became involved with my life, he wasn't so sure
about me teaching men in any setting. That is just the place where
he was in those days. When he tells this story, he says, "I
thumped my Bible and told Michal Ann, 'Now listen, (with a re-
sounding thump) this isn't right! You can't do this. This is against
the Word' (thump)."

To his amazement, I submitted. I resigned from my teaching
duties at the church and began to spend more time with Jim and his
circle of friends and fellowship at that time. We were walking in
the light or understanding that we had in those days, trying our
best to please God. Some years later, I went through a period of
time when I looked closely at the "head covering" issue, and whenever I joined Jim to pray for people, I'd wear a hat or covering of
some kind. Why? It was our conviction at the time concerning

issues of authority and of demonstrating a correct biblical posture toward the angels.

We have another understanding today. As Jim sometimes states, "My wife didn't have a head covering on the night the angels came to our bedroom. But they came powerfully anyway!" Now, we are not trying to change your convictions on head coverings. That is not our message. The heart is the issue. Right relationship with God and one another is the issue. Being secure with God and each other and releasing one another into the fullness of His plan and purposes is the issue.

Still Changing After All These Years...

We have been through countless issues like this that have required radical change in our lives. We're *still* dealing with issues of change, and so is the Church around the world. The angelic visitations in our home came to us long before God came to Toronto with the "Father's blessing," or descended in His glory on an Assemblies of God church in Pensacola, Florida. The visitations had nothing to do with our personal worth, pride, or personal agenda. We believe that the Lord was giving us a precursor or preview of what He wanted to do with His Bride, the Body of Christ.

As I mentioned before, from the first time I received a visitation from God to now, Jim and I have been stretched by the Spirit of God to *change*. Jim remembers receiving a word from the Lord in October of 1993 in which the Lord said, "I will keep coming upon you with waves of My Presence until I make you into a wild man." Yet throughout much of that period of time, God wasn't primarily speaking to Jim; He was speaking to me. That meant poor Jim had to make some major adjustments in his life. He describes those days this way:

> "God was speaking during this period of time to my wife, my bride. I was the pastor, the priest, the king, the prophet. But now, comparatively speaking, I was getting 'nothin',' honey.' The heavenly pipeline was opened to my wife, and

I had to learn that if I was now going to hear from God, I was going to have to hear the voice of the Lord *through my wife*.

"Now I don't want to paint you a picture that we fit totally into such a stereotyped image, because it wasn't that I never thought that God could speak to women. I'm painting this scene from our past to show you the life-changing effect that this prophetic event had on our relationship and ministry. The Lord was revealing His jealousy for His Bride. What was happening in our home and marriage as God raised up Michal Ann was soon going to happen in His Church. This was a pictorial preview of what the Holy Spirit was going to be doing with all of us, His Church—His Bride."

The issue was not simply the change that God demanded of us. The prophetic event of our angelic visitations in the night foreshadowed the way God wanted to come upon His Church. This message is for the entire Body of Christ, but it is of particular importance for women and for young people who often feel disqualified for service to God because of their gender or age. God wants to release His Spirit, love, and compassion on *all flesh*, because He is jealous for them. When God sees a husband and wife, or a family of five, or a youth group, He doesn't just speak to the husband or the youth pastor and say, "Now you tell your wife...now you tell those young people...." No, God wants to pull each individual aside and personally whisper His heart's desire for his or her life into his or her spirit.

Jim said that one of the most remarkable things the Lord ever said to him about me was this: "Before she was ever yours, she was Mine." That is true for every one of us. Before we ever belonged to anyone else, we were His first, and we will always be His first.

The Holy Spirit encounters I experienced in my bedroom over that nine-week period were primarily concerned with the jealousy of God. God is jealous for us, as His priests and His people. His jealousy begins long before we are born and will continue for eternity. Why? Because we belong to Him. We were literally created for His pleasure, and the fact is that He takes great delight in us as His children.

Three Angels and Our Son Tyler

A beautiful picture of God's jealousy or possessive love for us is illustrated in our third child, Tyler. As with each of us, Tyler was in the heart of God long before the possibility of his conception and birth was even in our thoughts. Long before he was born, the word of the Lord came to us one night as we were asleep. It was a calm fall night in September 1987 when a strong wind suddenly blew through our bedroom window. It blew open our door and proceeded out into the hallway, only to turn around, blow our door back shut with a slam, and whirl right back out of our bedroom window. We both instantly sat up in bed and realized that visitors of a heavenly kind were on the scene. The voice of the Holy Spirit declared, "I have come to give you commands concerning My last-day order." He also spoke concerning Tyler's conception. It was time for Tyler.

Because my two previous pregnancies were so difficult, Jim was very content to have our first two children, Justin and GraceAnn, and no more. He did not want to see me suffer anymore with childbearing. But when this word of the Lord came, the Lord instantly took away all fear and apprehension out of Jim's heart and replaced it with faith. Jim now *knew* we were to have a son, named Tyler, and he now had a tremendous surge of love deposited in his heart for Tyler. His heart and his mind were changed in an instant! While Jim was receiving this word, I saw something swirling over the bed. It seemed like a huge bird with a wing span of approximately 12 feet. I could feel its wings hovering about five feet over us. Jim could actually see three glistening forms that came and appeared, one at a time, at the end of our bed. These angels had the appearance of men who were dressed in military uniforms.

When the third angel came to the foot of the bed and looked at Jim, he thought the angel looked familiar, almost like a family relative. This angel was dressed in a modern military uniform, while the other angels were dressed in older uniforms from the Revolutionary War and the Civil War, respectively. Later that morning, the Lord gave Jim several different prophetic insights concerning Israel and world events that would come to pass in the 1990s and beyond, before the visitations ended. When Jim and I talked about this visitation later on, we began to suspect that the third angel was possibly a representation of the guardian angel of our future son, Tyler Hamilton.

Nine and a half months later, at 1:17 in the morning, Jim was deep in intercessory prayer in our living room concerning a historic prayer gathering occurring in Berlin, Germany. (I was asleep but uncomfortable because I was two weeks past due in my third pregnancy.) While Jim was interceding in our living room, this "third angel" from the visitation months before once again came to stand at the end of the room. He moved to the doorway and began to speak to Jim in the living room, saying, "It's time for Tyler Hamilton to be born; you must go and lay hands upon your wife and call him forth!"

Well, Just Do It!

Jim came into the room and woke me up to announce, "Ann, Tyler's angel has come. He has said to me, 'It is time for Tyler Hamilton to be born; you must go and lay hands upon your wife and call him forth.'"

I confess that I wasn't feeling especially "spiritual" in that moment. I felt that the Lord had spoken to me earlier that day, telling me that Tyler's birth was imminent and to get all the rest I could that day. So I was not surprised when Jim came in and told me his news. True rest is something difficult to get when you're nine-plus months pregnant and you have two other young children. I knew that the only way out was to go through the delivery process. I was tired and groggy, and anxious to see our son Tyler. So I said, "Well, just do it." My blunt response shocked Jim somewhat, but he went straight to his assignment and laid his hands on my stomach. (It was protruding quite a distance at that point.) Then Jim thundered his infamous words, "Tyler Hamilton, this is the voice of your father speaking. Your angel has just come and he said, 'It is time for Tyler Hamilton to be born; you must go and lay hands upon your wife and call him forth.' " And once again he said, "Tyler Hamilton, this is the voice of your father speaking. Listen and obey."

After Jim prayed, contractions started immediately. Some 18 hours of hard labor later, and what we felt was spiritual warfare, Tyler Hamilton Goll was born into the world. We weren't the least bit surprised to discover that this little wonder has a warrior anointing on his life. He's a fighter and a warrior, and like all parents, we need God's grace as we shape and mold him into the man of God he is ordained to become.

Just as God took intense interest in every aspect of Tyler's conception and birth, He also cares intensely and passionately for you and your destiny. I believe that the anointing we have seen flowing out of places like Pasadena, California; Pensacola, Florida; Smithton, Missouri; South America; England; Australia; and countless other places around the world will just keep increasing. The Lord is saying through these supernatural events, "I am coming with My jealousy to possess My people. I will keep coming with My Presence upon them to demonstrate My jealousy and great love for My Bride."

Take the Intimacy Plunge

Jim tells me that I *looked different* after God began to visit me in the night. We had a family portrait taken during the time of those visitations, and Jim and others firmly believe that those photos reveal a new intensity, or even an "ethereal" quality to them that wasn't there prior to my supernatural encounters with the fire of God. In hindsight, I can tell you that my entire life has been changed forever by those times of divine intimacy. God wants to visit His Church in the same way. He wants to visibly demonstrate His jealousy for His Bride and release His people—great and small, loud and quiet, bold and meek—into supernatural ministry rooted in intimacy with Him. We need to be committed to this journey to intimacy with God. We need to "take the intimacy plunge."

Jim had a dream concerning a "scrapbook" that was thrown in his lap, labeled "1988-89" on the front cover. The years themselves had prophetic meaning—eight is the number of a new beginning. Eight-eight is a year of the double, and 1988 was a time when the prophetic movement was breaking in Kansas City and in many places across the globe. He has no doubt about the meaning of the dream. As he thumbed through the pages of this scrapbook, he was surprised to see that the contents were depicting *covenants* and *vows* that people had made to the Lord during that period.

He turned to the page where his own name was written and read the covenant vow he apparently had made in this dream. It said, "I, Jim Goll, vow to be all that I can be in God. I vow to be the unique vessel that God has created me to be. I vow to help others be all that they can be in God, and I vow to help others be the unique vessels God has created them to be." The line that stood out the most to him was separate from the others, and it said in large capital letters:

"I vow to be a BRAVEHEART for God."

That is what this book is all about. God is looking for a people of passionate pursuit after Him. God seeks those who seek Him. When Jim woke from his dream, he was exhilarated. Of course, we are all aware of the Academy Award-winning film, *Braveheart*. When it was released, we thought, *Being a braveheart is an award-winning demonstration of the life of God*. Let's each be bravehearts for our God!

Our motto as bravehearts for the Lord should be this: "*I'm not who I was, and I'm not who I'm going to be, but I'm on the path of becoming*." I urge you to take a bold step of faith and venture out into this awesome, tremendous, and yet fearful journey with God. The Gospel of John offers us a glimpse of our appearance on this path of God in the verse that says, "The wind blows where it wishes and you hear the sound of it, but do not know where it comes from and where it is going; so is everyone who is born of the Spirit" (Jn. 3:8).

The Lord wants to blow away all the self-imposed controls that have entangled our lives. He wants to blow away our fear of men, our fear of breaking traditions, and our fear of repercussions. He wants us to be all that He wants us to be.

The Velvet Warriors

Recently Jim and I were at one of Randy Clark's conference where he began to minister about waging war with the prophetic. Jim saw a prophetic picture in his mind and began to sing a prophetic song. I joined him and we began to sing together about "the velvet warriors, the velvet army on its knees." Jim explained that he saw advancement coming in the Kingdom of God, but it wasn't a picture of troops running forward with great spears. He saw an army of velvet warriors marching forward by *crawling on their knees*. They were clothed in humility, mirroring dependency on God, but they were valiant warriors in the Lord.

Whenever I hear Jim talk about his visionary vow to be a "braveheart" for God, it reminds me of my season of extended angelic visitations. More than anything else, my supernatural encounters whetted my appetite for something that I had not tasted before. When the visitations began to come less frequently, I actually felt like I was lovesick. I found words to express my pain when I read this passage in the Song of Solomon:

> *I opened to my beloved, but my beloved had turned away and had gone! My heart went out to him as he spoke. I searched for him, but I did not find him; I called him, but he did not answer me. ... I adjure you, O daughters of Jerusalem, if you find my beloved, as to what you will tell him: for I am lovesick* (Song of Solomon 5:6,8).

The Lord has given us invitation after invitation to come into a place of intimacy with Him. This is a place were you must *press* in for Him. You press in because He is pressing in toward you at the same time. The mystery of the gospel is the mystery of a divine, eternal love story. It is all about capturing our hearts. It's all about wooing us into the place where nothing else matters but walking and being with God in unbroken fellowship. Walking in the Spirit has little to do with a bunch of head knowledge alone. It has everything to do with a heart response of waking up and knowing that your Bridegroom is calling. He is calling for His Bride, and He's fighting for His Bride. He ardently loves His Bride, and He is asking us to be mirrors of His perfect image, mirrors of Himself. He longs for us to be valiant warriors for His sake, people who are so in love with Him that no cost is too great!

The Time Has Come

About halfway through those blessed weeks in the fall of 1992, I had a pivotal experience. His Presence was overwhelming. I was having all kinds of dreams and experiences, feeling things, sensing things. I was trying to write everything down, trying not to miss anything. There was so much I did not understand at the time. It was becoming like a large mountain, overwhelming me. I was trying to be as responsible as I knew how, and yet I felt like the mountain of revelation was beginning to overshadow the Revelator, Jesus Christ. Late one night I found myself saying, "If these encounters do not bring me closer to Jesus and more in love with my Father, then what use are they? What are they for?" Quickly, the dove of God assured me, "That is exactly what they are for!"

I have a word for you. It is simple, yet profound and clear. Our God is a God of love; a God of strength and power. His great desire is toward you—His beloved Bride. Yes, pursue the God of visitation, not the visitations of God. Seek the God of power, not the power of God. Let's keep first things first. But if He grants you extraordinary encounters, remember that their ultimate purpose is to reveal the person of Jesus Christ, bring you into a greater intimacy with the Father, and empower you to testify to others of His great love!

Hosea 6:1-3 says it like this:

Come and let us return to the Lord, for He has torn so that He may heal us; He has stricken so that He may bind us up. After two days He will revive us (quicken us, give us life); on the third day He will raise us up that we may live before Him. Yes, let us know (recognize, be acquainted with, and understand) Him; let us be zealous to know the Lord [to appreciate, give heed to, and cherish Him]. His going forth is prepared and certain as the dawn, and He will come to us as the [heavy] rain, as the latter rain that waters the earth (AMP).

It is time for us to pursue the God of our visitation. It is time for His latter rain to water the earth. When you really love someone, when your heart is sold out 100 percent, then there is nothing you wouldn't do for your beloved. No task is too difficult. This is the ultimate and most important goal of all supernatural encounters. It is time for us to give our all for Him who gave His all for us. Let us pursue the God of visitations, and may close encounters with a supernatural God begin!

A Closing Prayer

Father God, I present myself to You. I believe that Jesus Christ is Your great and only Son. I come to present myself, my family, and my future to You. I need You more than I have ever needed You before! Come, Holy Spirit! Come and invade my unholy comfort zones with the love of God. Change me. Shape me. Drive fear and unbelief out of me. Consume me with the fire of Your holy Presence. I welcome Your ambassadors, the angels of the Lord, to do Your bidding. Take control of my life. Bring me close encounters of a heavenly kind. For Your holy name's sake! Amen.

Destiny Image
New Releases

THE LOST ART OF INTERCESSION
by Jim W. Goll.
How can you experience God's anointing power as a result of your own prayer? Learn what the Moravians discovered during their 100-year prayer Watch. They sent up prayers; God sent down His power. Jim Goll, who ministers worldwide through a teaching and prophetic ministry, urges us to heed Jesus' warning to "watch." Through Scripture, the Moravian example, and his own prayer life, Jim Goll proves that "what goes up must come down."
ISBN 1-56043-697-2 $9.99p

USER FRIENDLY PROPHECY
by Larry J. Randolph.
Hey! Now you can learn the basics of prophecy and how to prophesy in a book that's written for you! Whether you're a novice or a seasoned believer, this book will stir up the prophetic gift God placed inside you and encourage you to step out in it.
ISBN 1-56043-695-6 $9.99p

FOR GOD'S SAKE GROW UP!
by David Ravenhill.
It's time to grow up...so that we can fulfill God's purposes for us and for our generation! For too long we've been spiritual children clinging to our mother's leg, refusing to go to school on the first day. It's time to put away childish things and mature in the things of God—there is a world that needs to be won to Christ!
ISBN 1-56043-299-3 $9.99p

WORSHIP: THE PATTERN OF THINGS IN HEAVEN
by Joseph L. Garlington.
Joseph Garlington, a favorite Promise Keepers' speaker and worship leader, delves into Scripture to reveal worship and praise from a Heaven's-eye view. Learn just how deep, full, and anointed God intends our worship to be.
ISBN 1-56043-195-4 $9.99p

Available at your local Christian bookstore.

Internet: http://www.reapernet.com

Prices subject to change without notice.   2:93

MTTN RESOURCES

TAPES BY MICHAL ANN GOLL

Visitations in the Night . . . . .A2VIN $10.00
Casting Off Every Weight . . . . .A2CEW $10.00
Women in the Prophetic . . . . .DG24B $5.00
 Video (960713V10) $15.00
Prophetic Dreams .GB3B $5.00
Women of Courage . . . . .HD5F $5.00
Annie Get Your Gun . . . . .GE03A $5.00
No More Fear! . . . . .GE11A $5.00
Burden of the Heart . . . . .HD4D $5.00
Putting on the Helmet of Hope . . . . .HJ10A $5.00
 Video (971010V1) $15.00
Loveliness of Loneliness . . . . .EC05G $5.00
B-29 Bombers . . . . .FE13D $5.00

TAPES BY JIM W. GOLL

Dream Language . . . . .A2DLG $10.00
Levels of Supernatural Visions . . . . .A2LSU $10.00
 Video (961004VB-1) $15.00
Interpreting Dreams and Revelations . . . . .A2IDR $10.00
Varieties of Prophetic Anointings . . . . .A3VPA $15.00
Angelic Encounters .A4AES $20.00
Trances: A Biblical View . . . . .A2TBV $10.00
Releasing Creativity . . . . .GF22B $5.00
 Video (960713V7) $15.00
The Deception of the Anointing . . . . .EF15A $5.00
Seven Expressions of the Prophetic Spirit .BG14B $5.00
 Video (961004V7) $15.00
Hearing God's Voice . . . . .FK01A $5.00
How to Receive Revelation . . . . .GC16A $5.00
Judging Revelation .AC06A $5.00
Pits and Pinnacles of Prophetic Ministry . .FF17B $5.00
 Video (950617V8) $15.00

Send your order information with check made payable to:

Ministry to the Nations
P.O. Box 338
Antioch, TN 37011-0338

Or fax credit card orders to:
(615) 365-4408 or **(615) 365-4401** M-F 9-4 p.m.

Or order from our website at: **http://www.reapernet.com/mttn**

Visa, MasterCard, and personal checks are accepted.
A shipping and handling charge will be applied to your order.